Son of a Sharecropper

Son of a Sharecropper

◆

Growing Up in Oklahoma 1913–1940

Dave H. Roper
with David L. Roper

iUniverse, Inc.
New York Lincoln Shanghai

Son of a Sharecropper
Growing Up in Oklahoma 1913–1940

iUniverse, Inc.

For information address:
iUniverse, Inc.
2021 Pine Lake Road, Suite 100
Lincoln, NE 68512
www.iuniverse.com

ISBN: 0-595-32106-2

Printed in the United States of America

Dedicated to Lillian Irene (Dacus) Roper
My wife and companion of almost seventy years

Contents

1

"ONCE UPON A TIME"
1913–1917

1913 was a momentous year. Woodrow Wilson was president of America. The U. S. income tax law went into effect. Henry Ford established the automobile assembly line. A German professor announced a new diphtheria serum. A postage stamp cost 2¢, a loaf of bread 6¢, and a quart of milk 9¢. Oklahoma had enjoyed statehood for six years. Of special significance were those born that year. Among them: Richard Nixon, Danny Kaye, Jesse Owens, Burt Lancaster...and Dave H. Roper.

Once upon a time (that's the way all stories should start), the year after the sinking of the Titanic, a young couple in their mid-twenties lived in a log cabin in a tree-covered region of eastern Oklahoma. The cabin was three miles east of Beebe, a small country oil town that has since disappeared.

The couple—Lee Barney and Maud Alice (Cruzan) Roper—were honest, hard-working, happy people. They had two lovely daughters: Hazel Lorene, born April 28, 1908; and Hester Viola, born June 22, 1911. But Lee wanted a son to carry on the family name. Finally, on October 5, 1913, it happened.

My birth was the do-it-yourself variety common to that day: little fanfare and no doctor, nurse, or hospital—not even a midwife. Just a couple of nervous, excited parents doing what has been done millions of times since Adam and Eve: bringing another small member into the human race. The birthing went well and everybody survived.

I was a blond-headed, blue-eyed baby, weighing in at about ten pounds. I was named Lee David Hamilton Roper after my father (*Lee* Barney Roper) and both grandfathers (*Hamilton* "Hampy" Greenberry Roper and *David* Logan Cruzan). When I was young, I was generally called "Son." I was called D. H. or "Dick" through high school. Eventually, I became Dave H. Being the first boy and having two older sisters, there are those who claim I was spoiled in my early years: a rumor started by the jealous.

My father was probably a share-cropper on the farm on which the cabin was located. Sometimes Dad rented the land, but usually he had a share-crop arrangement. There were two kinds of share-crop arrangements: If we furnished the labor and the landowner furnished everything else—the land, the seed, the horses, and the equipment—he got half of all our crops. If all he furnished was the land, he got one-fourth of the cotton and one-third of the feed crop. Either way, it was hard to scrape by on what was left after the landowner got his share. I wasn't very old before one of my dreams was to own land.

I also wanted a good barn full of hay. And a horse to ride. One of my earliest memories is wanting to own a horse. After all, how can you be a Roper without a horse? But I'm getting ahead of my story.

I have only vague memories of my first few years, but my older sisters have filled in some of the blanks for me. According to them, Son soon began to demand attention. He would stir up the household at midnight yelling for food, or crying at 5:00 a.m. for a change of diapers. The diapers of that day were three-cornered pieces of cloth we called "diaties." The throw-away variety was still far in the future. These diaties were cleaned by use of a rub board and hard scrubbing with lye soap. They were then boiled in an iron pot and rinsed in cold water. Afterward they were hung on a fence to dry.

My loving parents didn't believe in spoiling their kids, but (according to my older siblings) I got just about what I wanted when I wanted it. Which was only fair since I was the first boy and heir apparent. Fortunately, being the almost perfect baby, I didn't take to spoiling.

The little cabin soon became too small for the growing family. So the wagon bows were put on the wagon, the wagon sheet adjusted, the few old hens put in a wire coop and swung under the wagon, our meager belongings loaded, and we traveled westward. This was the first of many moves I would make over the next 90 years. My oldest sister, Hazel, wrote about that move and related matters:

When D. H. was a tiny baby, we moved to a 40-acre farm three miles north of Stratford. It had a two-room house on it. It was all woods and had to be cleared before it could be farmed. Glen Biles helped Papa clear the land.

Glen and Iva Biles and their children stayed with us a lot. There was always someone staying with us. It never seemed to bother Mother to have someone with us.

One day, I was loving D. H. while he was on Mother's lap. Hester said, "You don't love me." I said, "I'm supposed to love him because he is a baby."

Before we moved off our 40-acre farm, I remember we went to church at a school house one Sunday morning in a wagon. My mother went to the front and prayed. She was a member of the Church of Christ. We didn't go to church often because there wasn't a church around there.

We went on a vacation before we moved from our 40-acre farm. We went in a covered wagon and enjoyed it so much. Mother sat on the wagon seat and drew so many interesting things. We went to Mother's sister's place in western Oklahoma. Papa got a job for a while. We lived in an empty house with just a bed and a stove. Mother made bread called light bread. She put it on the floor near stove to rise. D. H. was learning to walk and stepped in it. (Poor baby!)

MY MOTHER

My mother was born January 25, 1887, in Texas—the daughter of David Logan and Amy Jane (Plew) Cruzan. She and my father were married July 7, 1907, at Byars, Oklahoma. I don't remember much about my mother, but I have pictures of her. And I have her diary and the memories of others. Apparently she was a beautiful, talented young woman and a loving mother. It is not hard to imagine this pioneer woman busy with daily chores, such as...

- Taking care of the children, cooking the meals, and keeping the house clean.
- Washing clothes on the rub board and ironing with sad irons (AKA flat irons which were heated on the stove).
- Patching clothes and making a few garments on a treadle sewing machine.
- Making a garden, canning and drying vegetables, and making hominy.
- Making jelly from wild grapes and plums—and preserving other fruit if any was available. Fruit was spread on top of the house for drying,.

- Feeding the chickens and gathering the eggs.
- Milking the cow and churning butter.
- Slopping the pigs.

Speaking of pigs, once a year was hog-killing. Then she had the messy jobs of rendering the lard in the old black wash pot, grinding the sausage, and making the year's supply of lye soap.

MY FATHER

Dad will be constantly mentioned in this book, but a few introductory notes would not be out of order: He was born August 27, 1885, near Gassville in Baxter County, Arkansas, the son of "Hampy" and Ada (Mooney) Roper. When he was a lad, his family moved to Wise County, Texas. After a few years, in 1898, they moved to Indian Territory. He grew up in and around Garvin County.

Dad was a quiet man—didn't talk much. He was a gentle man, although he did get riled once in a while. He was witty—at least half. He grinned a lot, but one of the great events of the year was when "Papa laughed out loud!"

He was a hard worker. He was never happy loafing. He seldom went hunting or fishing unless it was to get food. He was honest and dependable, traits he passed on to his kids.

He had little formal education, but encouraged his kids to go to school as best he could. He was not much of a church-goer, but never objected to others' religion. He was a "mover"—always looking for something better.

About two years after I was born, another member was added to the family: my third sister, Janada, who was born November 14, 1915. Her name is a combination of the names of our grandmothers (Amy *Jane* Cruzan and Martha *Ada* Mooney). Of course I was proud of her and not a bit jealous as some might suppose. Because (remember) I was still the only boy and the heir apparent. As such, I still got my share of attention and more. So, with my mild manners and good looks, I took everything in stride.

PRESIDENTIAL MATERIAL?

As I think back on my early days, I wonder why I was never President:

- I was born in a log cabin.

- My mother died when I was four, and Dad married a widow with two children. Eventually, this union had a total of ten children.

- My family was honest and hard-working, share-croppers who moved almost every year.

- I picked cotton and pulled bolls. I plowed with horses behind a walking plow.

- I was raised without electricity or natural gas. I never lived in a house with running water or a bathroom until I was 19 years old. (The only running H2O we had was that which came through the holes in the roof.) Grandma had a party-line telephone, but my family never had a phone.

- I never had a store-bought haircut until I was married (age 20). It cost 25¢.

- I was a "womanizer": There have been four women in my life—my mother, my stepmother, my grandmother, and my wife.

- I have "a criminal record": I played hooky from school; I smoked corn silks and grape vines; I was a gambler (playing "keeps" with marbles and pitching pennies); I once carried a pistol to school in my boot; and I was guilty of arson (I started a forest fire).

If at least some of the above does not qualify me to be President, I don't know what would. At least I should run for Congress.

2

WORLD WAR I—
AND THE FLU
1917–1918

In 1914, the fragile peace in Europe was broken, but President Woodrow Wilson was determined to keep the U. S. out of the war. In 1915, the British liner Lusitania was sunk by a German submarine and 114 Americans drowned; it was a turning point in national sentiment. In 1916, Wilson campaigned on the slogan "He kept us out of the war." In 1917, the start of Wilson's second term, the U. S. declared war on Germany.

More than 90,000 Oklahomans served in the Armed Forces during World War I.

When I was four years old, we lived on a farm northeast of Stratford: the Cunningham place. This farm was one mile east and one mile north of McGee school. It had a nice house with a lovely fireplace, and it also had a good barn. The Graves were the nearest neighbors, about a half mile away. You could see their house from where we lived.

THE FLU EPIDEMIC OF 1918

The U. S. entered World War I April 6, 1917. The fighting was still going on in 1918, the year of the great world-wide flu epidemic. Twenty-one million people died worldwide. I believe the flu bug was brought back from Europe by returning military men. Sometimes people died so fast that it was hard to find enough well people to bury the dead.

In the country and small towns, there was nothing resembling a funeral home. The deceased were laid out by loving hands of neighbors or relatives. They moved the body, bathed and dressed it in the best clothes they had, and put the body on a table or bed until burying time—which was usually the next day. Neighbor men got together and dug the grave by hand. They never asked or received money for the job. If the family had money and a casket was available, they secured it, but often the casket was made by friends. The night before the funeral, some friends or relatives sat up with the body all night. The day of the funeral, if there was a church building close enough, they might have the funeral service there. Otherwise, the casket was loaded on a wagon and driven to the graveyard where the service was held. After the sermon, the casket was lowered into the grave by four men—two on each side—using check lines from a harness as a lowering device.

THE DEATH OF MY MOTHER

February 2, 1918, my mother had her fifth child, a boy named Kenneth. In April, she died of flu and pneumonia, leaving a husband with five children (the youngest was two-months-old Kenneth). She was buried in the McGee cemetery near Stratford, Oklahoma. Concerning Mom's death, my sister Hazel, wrote,

> Mother wasn't very strong. She had weak lungs. She had had pneumonia twice, and the doctor said that if she had pneumonia again, it would kill her.

She had a baby boy, Kenneth, and when he was three days old, she had flu and pneumonia. She passed away early in 1918.

I remember an ugly boy in school making fun of me because my mother died. When he grew up, he married one of my friends, but he was still ugly.

Jake and Ada Dacus were neighbors, and Ada helped lay out the body and prepare it for burial. Jake was an uncle of the woman who later became my wife—but of course that was far in the future.

Shortly after the death of my mother, our grandparents, Hampy and Ada Roper, took us in. They lived about one mile from us (cross country) on their old home place. Clyde, Papa's youngest brother, still lived at home; he was about sixteen years old. Aunt Zealin, Papa's baby sister, was also there; she was about ten years old. So we had a family of ten people living in a three-room house. Papa continued to farm the Cunningham place that year.

A GREAT LADY

I'll be saying a lot about Grandma Roper through this book. They broke the mold when they finished her. At least her young grandson thought so. But let me go ahead and tell you a bit about her.

Martha Ada Mooney was born November 26, 1868, in Baxter County, Arkansas, the daughter of George Clayton and Amelia (Williams) Mooney. She married Hamilton G. Roper March 21, 1883, in Baxter County—and they made the move to Wise County, Texas, and finally to Indian Territory.

Like most of their ancestors, Grandma and Grandpa were farmers. Farming was a busy way of life and Grandma was always working. "A woman's work is never done" surely applied to her. After feeding the family breakfast (all ten of us), she would milk old Brindle, the family cow. She made all the butter and cottage cheese, and did most of the gardening.

In the summer, she was busy canning and drying peaches and apples. She picked berries on the halves for canning. She gathered wild grapes and plums for jelly-making. In between these jobs, she supervised the incubator and took care of the setting hens and baby chicks.

Then there was the weekly wash, no small job for ten people. She would draw water from the well and fill the large iron pot. After rubbing the clothes on the rub board, they would be put in the pot to boil. No germs could live through that! Finally, the clothes were rinsed and hung up to dry.

Grandma firmly believed that "idle hands were the devil's workshop," so she kept everybody busy at something. Inside the house, she was the dominant figure. She kept things moving and everybody busy. One yell from Grandma in the morning and all us kids hit the floor, dressed for the day. In a few minutes, we were all seated at the table and ready to eat as soon as the blessing was said. There was no complaining about the food. It was "Clean your plate"—and keep your mouth shut—while you were eating.

Grandma was a sincere, religious woman who practiced what she preached. I can still hear her singing "In the Sweet Bye and Bye" and the "Lily of the Valley" as she went about her daily chores. She always said grace before meals. She believed she ought to meet with the saints on Sunday, if possible, and that you ought to dress properly. She always dressed in her Sunday best with white gloves and hat. When grandkids were visiting, there was no question about attending. You went with Grandma leading the way.

It may have been Grandma who taught me the child's prayer:

Now I lay me down to sleep.
I pray the Lord my soul to keep.
If I should die before I wake,
I pray the Lord my soul to take.

Few nights have gone by the last eighty years that I have not repeated those words.

Grandma had strong convictions about the word "sin." She was quick to teach about what she considered right or wrong. Grandma believed that what the Good Book said in the Old Testament about wearing "clothes pertaining to a man" still applied. She always wore a dress. Dancing was an evil Grandma abhorred. She was convinced that it was invented by the devil himself. She wouldn't allow "face cards" in the house; they were used for gambling.

One of the sins she hated most was drinking whiskey—and rightly so. She lost two sons to Demon Rum. One son was a part-time moonshiner who died at age twenty-eight because of drinking poisoned whisky. At least that's what Grandma thought. The other died on a dark rainy night, crossing the street in a drunken stupor. He was less than fifty years old. I heard her say many times, "If I'm dying and whisky will save me, let me die!"

When Grandma came to visit us, she always brought her needle and lots of thread. First she would gather up all the dirty clothes and wash and iron them. Then she went through them, darning socks, sewing on buttons, patching holes—fixing whatever needed fixing. Her motto: "Maybe you can't help being poor, but you can be clean and patched."

She was a great believer in Jesus words: "It's more blessed to give than to receive." Trouble was that she wanted to get all the blessings; she wanted to do all the giving. There was no way you could out-give Grandma! When we visited her, we always left with a lot more than we came with. She would always fill up the wagon or the car with all kinds of goodies—like fresh vegetables, canned fruit, dried fruit, or maybe a ham or a dozen eggs—or even a quilt if you needed it.

It was a treat to go to Grandma's house on Christmas. She always boiled a large fresh ham the day before, outside in a large black wash pot. After cooking it all day, she would remove the skin and surplus fat and spot the ham all over with black pepper. It was not only colorful but so delicious.

GRANDPA HAMPY

I should also say a few words about Grandpa Hampy. His name was Hamilton
Greenberry Roper, but everyone called him "Hampy." He was born December 1,

1862, in Baxter County, Arkansas, the son of Peter Byrum and Nancy Jane (Cape) Roper. He was about fifty-five when we went to live with them. He was a small man, about 5' 6" tall, weighing around 120 pounds, with a slightly humped back.

He had brown hair. He still had a full head of hair when he died in his seventies. He also had a bushy moustache. I never saw him without his upper lip covered. Grandma said that Grandpa went on a trip once and shaved his moustache off. On returning, she didn't recognize him and refused to let him in the house. When she finally recognized him, she let him in the house on the condition he wouldn't shave it off again.

He never wore glasses and never had false teeth. He also never owned a car and never learned to drive.

I remember Grandpa as a very quiet person. He was pretty much a loner and had few close friends. It didn't seem to bother him to be by himself. He was apparently content to let Grandma do the talking if she was around. It wasn't as if he was too bashful to talk. I think he worked on the principle "You don't learn by talking but by listening." The world would probably be better off if we had more people with that philosophy

He was a hard-worker. He was up before sunup and went to bed with the chickens. Each morning, Grandpa was first one up. He kept the wood box full, and then got up every morning and built the fires. He had a chronic cough. I can still hear him whooping and coughing while he built fires on a cold morning. After he built the fire, while Grandma was getting breakfast, he would feed the horses and get ready to head for the field. Grandma never built a fire and Grandpa never milked a cow. Apparently he thought milking cows was woman's work.

Grandpa worked hard to provide for his family. I remember seeing him come from the field, his clothes wringing wet with sweat. I wanted to get big so I could sweat like Grandpa! Being the only small boy, I received special privileges like going to the field at the close of the day and riding home on the horses. Also, at times, Gramps would let me drive the team as we rode to town in the wagon. How big I felt!

Grandpa was honest and respected by his peers. And he liked kids. I can't remember him ever being fussy with us. He wasn't one to show a lot of affection but we knew he would help us if needed. Being the only grandson at home, he took me with him on occasion to cut wood, make molasses, and go hunting.

He and Grandma raised a family of nine children. Seven lived to maturity. My father, being the oldest, was honored by his parents by being nicknamed "Brother." They always called him by that name.

To my knowledge, Grandpa never claimed any type of religion, but he never interfered nor objected to church-going. Grandma set the religion tone for the whole family. Grandpa would take Grandma to the meetings but very few times do I remember him going inside the building or the brush-arbor. His religion seemed to be "Love your neighbor" and help people as needed. I guess it could be said of him (like some say today) that he was "spiritual, but not religious."

THE TOBACCO KING OF OKLAHOMA

Did I mention that Grandpa smoked a pipe? One incident I remember about him was when he had his own tobacco patch. Grandpa was always saying, "I'm out of tobacco." And Grandma would say, "If you'd grow your own, you wouldn't always be running out." Thus was born the idea of Grandpa's tobacco patch.

Grandpa sent off for tobacco seed and started cleaning a small patch of new ground close to his house. To grow tobacco, the ground had to be very clean, so he cut, raked, and burned all the brush and weeds from the seed bed. When the seeds arrived, he carefully planted them. To be sure that they sprouted, he carried water from the well and thoroughly saturated the soil.

Oklahoma is not known as a tobacco-growing state, so Grandpa was very excited about his project. Every day he would examine the seed bed, anxiously awaiting the arrival of the tiny plants. Sure enough, the plants finally broke through the soil. After being watered and tenderly nurtured for several days, the plants were removed and set out in the tobacco patch. They were very small, but so important to Grandpa. This was a great adventure; he was introducing a new crop to Oklahoma. Anytime the question was asked, "Where's Grandpa?" the answer was "He's in the tobacco patch."

All summer long, he was busy: hoeing weeds or picking off tobacco worms. He was like a kid with a new toy. He was probably thinking, "I'll be the tobacco king of Oklahoma."

By September, the plants had grown and matured to a height of three or four feet. It was harvest time! What a thrill! "My own tobacco. No more trips to the grocery store to get tobacco. No more nicotine fits because I'm out of tobacco."

The stalks were cut. The lower leaves were removed and the stalks were hung upside down in the barn to dry and cure.

Finally, Grandpa was able to enjoy the fruits of his labor. Through the fall and winter months, he had his home-grown tobacco. By springtime, the tobacco was gone and all that was left were the bare stalks hanging in the barn. Did he spend hours in contemplation whether it was worth the effort? To the best of my knowledge, he never grew any more.

THE DAY GRANDMA FAILED TO DO HER JOB

Back to 1918: As already mentioned, when I was at Grandma and Grandpa's house, I generally received special treatment. Which introduces this incident:

I was four years old. Being the oldest boy, I felt that I should have special privileges—such as going with Dad wherever he went: to plow, to cut wood, or to town. Dad was patient with me and generally let me go. But there were a few times when Dad refused to let me go. Some of these times, Grandma tied me up so I wouldn't follow Dad. But it was bound to happen…a great awakening…a lesson still remembered.

Dad was getting ready to go to town—a great event at the time. I also started getting ready. But, much to my surprise, he said I couldn't go. I went in the other room, got my coat on, slipped out and got in the back seat of the Model T touring car. Shortly, here came Dad. He told me to get out, that I wasn't going. I sat dumb-founded. Dad reached over, picked me up, and gave me three or four smacks where it hurt most (mainly it hurt my feelings).

After he drove off, I went crying to Grandma. "Grandma," I wailed, "why didn't you tie me up before Dad whipped me?" I still remember the day that Grandma failed to do her job.

CONTINUATION OF WORLD WAR I

The war continued through the summer and fall of that year. Papa got his notice from the draft board. It was raining the morning he left to appear for active duty. It was a sad day. "Papa's going to war," we thought. But after he reported and his family responsibilities noted, he was exempted and sent back home the same day.

The war brought on some shortages of food, one being flour. We ate lots of cornbread, but cornbread with gravy is no treat. Also, horses were conscripted for use in the cavalry, which was still an important part of the army. The army buyer would come to your farm and look at your horses. If they were what he wanted, he paid you for them and took them.

THE DEATH OF MY BROTHER

While we were staying with Grandpa and Grandma, Kenneth came down with measles and pneumonia. He died in May 1918, two months or so after mother died. He was buried in McGee Cemetery beside his mother.

The war ended November 11, 1918.

3

A NEW MOTHER—AND A FIGHTING GRANDMA 1919

In national news, the 18th amendment (the prohibition of liquor) was ratified in 1919. In 1919, in Oklahoma, James B. A. Robertson became the fourth governor of Oklahoma. He began to oppose the Ku Klux Klan that had flourished in the hectic days following the war.

A NEW MOTHER

Our closest neighbors, the Graves, had a daughter, Oren, in her late teens. Oren's husband, a full-blood Cherokee Indian named Sampson Lewis, had died from the flu, leaving her with a two-year-old boy, Sam (nickname, Rusty). Sam had been born September 10, 1917. Shortly after Sampson died, a second boy was born May 23, 1919: W. M. (sometimes called "Dub").

I might mention that since their father had been a full-blood Indian, the two boys had Indian rights. During the school year, they went to an Indian boarding school at Colony, Oklahoma. Generally, they were only home during the summer.

A little over a year after my mother's death, on July 18, 1919, Dad and Oren were married. At the time, there was considerable prejudice against Indians. My grandmother was not happy about the marriage. I don't think she ever really accepted Oren as a daughter.

Oren, nineteen years old at the time of the marriage, had six kids in her new family, from eight years (Hazel) to a few months (W. M.)! She had an impossible job! And my siblings and I didn't make it any easier. One time, Oren tried to discipline me. When she started toward me, I turned and ran. I ran into the field where Dad was plowing and stayed there all morning. I came in when Dad came

17

to dinner. I don't remember any more being said about it. Another time, when Oren tried to discipline Hester, Hazel jumped on her back.

Hazel especially didn't like her new stepmother. When she and Oren had disagreements, Hazel would bundle up her and her sisters' clothes in a sheet and take them through the woods to Grandma's house.

You have to feel sorry for Oren: not accepted by her mother-in-law, with rebellious stepchildren, and still just a kid herself. I say again that she had an impossible task. But she was a hard worker and sweet to be around.

A FIGHTING GRANDMA

After the wedding, we moved back to Cunningham house for the rest of that year. Once again my grandparents lived a mile away—through the woods. Which reminds me of another story:

One of the traits I admired about Grandma was her fighting spirit. She wasn't a big woman. As a matter of fact, she weighed just under the century mark. But she was always ready to defend what she believed to be right.

As previously noted, Grandma showed some partiality to me. She was quick to defend me in any squabbles I had with my three sisters. And she was always saying, "Son, I'd fight a tiger for you."

One day, when I was about 5 years old, Grandma was visiting at our house, and plans were made for me to spend the night with her. At last Grandma said, "We've got to be going. We want to be home before dark." But I found an excuse to put off the departure. After several extensions of time, Grandma became suspicious and asked, "Why are you not ready to go?"

Then the truth came out: "Grandma, you always say that you'd fight a tiger for me. I thought if we waited until dark, we might meet a tiger in the woods and I could see you fight him."

Grandma lived until I was thirty-six years of age, and I saw her conquer many foes. But I never did see her fight that tiger.

4

MUSIC, MOVING, AND MALARIA 1920

In 1920, women voted for the first time in the U. S., and America went dry as prohibition began. In Oklahoma, oil production flourished (the first producing oil well in Oklahoma had been drilled in 1889).

Occasionally I hear the cry "What can we do for fun?" How about a game of marbles? Why not spin a top? Or play mumbly peg? If you want something more vigorous, roll a hoop or ride a stick horse. I mentioned earlier my dream of owning my own horse. I still remember my first horse: Dad made me a beautiful stick horse from a willow tree. How proud I was! I mounted him with gusto and rode off into the wild blue (green?) yonder! For the next couple of years, I chased Indians and outlaws, and shot buffaloes and other varmints.

But stick horses may not appeal to you. Climbing trees is always an option, or playing cowboys and Indians. If you're an adult, try horseshoes. If you like crafts, make a bow and arrow or a corncob pipe. And there's always hunting and fishing (did you ever roust a rabbit out of a hollow log with a piece of barbed wire?) And, of course, there are always musical pursuits....

MY MUSICAL CAREER

When I was about 8 or 9, my Dad, an uncle, and I got in a wagon and drove to several deserted farmsteads, looking for scrap iron to sell. In the evening we drove to Stratford to sell it. My reward for helping was a fifty-cent harmonica. My first musical instrument and the beginning of a great career! The next few weeks, I literally blew the notes out of it—but I never quite managed a tune.

A few years later, when I was ten years old, I acquired a Jews Harp. That instrument lasted about two months. It made wonderful noises. But again, no musical tunes. A listing of other instruments I owned or tried to play would include a mandolin in high school and a baritone horn in college.

Years later, in a rural school near Grandview, Oklahoma, I was the director for the 3rd and 4th grade flutophone band. When we lived in Australia, I acquired my first guitar ($10.00). In 1994, while we were living on the farm near Pernell, I acquired my second guitar from my granddaughter Angi. Christmas that year I got another harmonica with taped instructions. As soon as I can find a recording company that appreciates my talents, I expect to put out my first CD.

But I'm getting ahead of my story. Back to 1920 and the exciting events in my life:

MOVING TIME

"Load em up! Move em out!" could have been the Roper motto. For some reason, the moving gene is overdeveloped in Ropers. One Roper genealogist says that, in his research, he has never found a Roper who died in the same place where he was born. We may not have been "shakers," but we were "movers."

The first of each year was moving time for us. The fiscal year was January 1 to January 1. If you rented a farm, you generally rented it January 1 to January 1. The thing I remember most is that we usually moved during the *coldest* part of the year. This may have added to my desire to own my own farm: Then I wouldn't have to move when it was freezing!

As a child, I remember the signs that moving time had come again: Dad greasing the wagon wheels and then putting up the bows and wagon sheet. We moved so often that when our chickens heard the word "move," they hopped up into the wagon and lay on their backs, their feet up in the air, ready to be tied. (OK, it's an old joke, but it fits.)

Moving days always had regrets: leaving familiar surroundings and old friends. It was kind of an adventure, too: We got to see new country, explore a new farm, and meet new people. But we also had to change schools, which I didn't like much because I was bashful and didn't make friends that easily.

Anyway, when January of 1920 rolled around, it was that time again. We loaded the wagon with all our earthly possessions (the family milk cow was tied to the back of the wagon) and headed east. Our family at the time consisted of six kids, a mother aged twenty, and a dad thirty-four.

We moved to a farm about twelve miles northwest of Ada, Oklahoma, a few miles from Beebe and about two miles from where I was born. Uncle Gladys (Papa's brother) and Aunt Annis lived a half mile or so from us.

We had a unique house. The original log house had one large room and a fireplace. In later years, a frame house had been built next to the log house, but the two were not connected. The frame house had one large room with a small lean-to side room. The log house was used for the kid's bedroom. The side room in the frame house was the kitchen, while the large room was the living room, dining room, and "master bedroom."

Dad rented the farm from "Aunt" Becky, an elderly (I thought) half-Indian widow who lived near our house. She lived alone in a nice two-room log house with a dog trot between the two rooms. Both rooms had a fireplace. We liked Aunt Becky and she seemed to like for us kids to visit her. I remember Aunt Becky's dough balls. She had a habit of taking a small amount of bread dough, making it into a ball about the size of a marble and continually rolling it around in her hand.

Since I had turned six the previous October, I started to school in September of 1920. I was pushed from the nest by loving parents who thought I needed some "book larnin." My two older sisters, Hazel and Hester, and I left that log cabin—sitting serenely in the South Canadian River bottom—and walked about a mile and a half to a one-room school called Woostal. Janada, the baby, had to stay at home. As best I can remember, I enjoyed my first days at school. As I started, little did I know that it would take me fifty years to get out of the classroom.

Memories of that year include Dad and Uncle Gladys seining fish in the South Canadian River. And baling hay: I drove the horses around and around so as to compress the hay—an ideal job for a six-year-old.

Our farm was about a mile from the river and we raised cotton on the rich bottom land. World War I was over—the Armistice had been signed near the end of 1918—and prices for farm produce were high. Cotton brought about 40¢ per pound. So, from an economic stand point, it was a good year. Papa made one of the few major purchases our family ever made: He bought an Edison gramophone—with the cylinder records. We were really up town!

THAT OLD COTTON PATCH

This is as good a place as any to say a few words about pulling cotton. We started pulling in late August or early September, depending on the weather—whenever the cotton bolls started poppin'. It was a time of excitement, a time when we could be thinking about a new pair of shoes or overalls or a pair of socks. Maybe even visualizing a beef roast and a loaf of store-bought bread.

As cotton sharecroppers, "prosperity" came once a year—at cotton harvest. Cotton was the only cash crop we had, so we were thrilled when that first bale of cotton was picked and hauled to the gin.

Cotton raising seemed like a 13-months-a-year job. You barely got it harvested until it was time to cut stalks and start plowing, planting, cultivating. And don't forget the hoeing. But we got a bit of respite in late summer when we would attend school for 4–5 weeks until the cotton was ready to pick.

When the cotton was ready, nothing, except the weather, interfered with the harvest. But it was a good time for us kids. We were out of school and could look forward to some spending money. The words "weekly allowance" had not been invented at that time. We had not heard about child labor laws. We didn't realize we were being abused, that our ego was suffering, or that we had a low self-esteem. We hadn't even heard of the ACLU. Raising cotton (not cane) was our way of life.

It was somewhat of a thrill to put that cotton sack on for the first time. We usually had to use some of the old sacks from the previous harvest for the first bale. When that first check came in, Dad would buy yards of ducking cloth and the lady of the house would get out the old Singer sewing machine and make new sacks. Sacks could be purchased ready-made, but they cost more so we always used the homemade variety.

The smaller sacks were about six feet long and the larger ones eight to twelve feet. The smaller kids used tow sacks. After the sacks were made, the shoulder straps were sewn on. A wire loop was twisted around one corner of the bottom of the sack so it could be hung on the scales.

I figure those cotton sacks did a lot of good for this old world. They kept kids busy and out of trouble. They bought food for the hungry and put clothes on their backs and shoes on their feet. They even bought books for learning. They have even helped people get to heaven. One day I was visiting a preacher and he said, "Come out to the garage." After we got there, he pointed to an old tattered and torn pick sack hanging on the wall, and said, "That's the reason I started preaching. I decided there was something more important than picking cotton.

Every time I think about quitting preaching, I look at that sack and head back to the pulpit."

About halfway through the season, the bottom side of the cotton sacks would be worn thin. It was time to take the straps off, turn the sacks over, and sew the straps back on. And keep on picking.

By the time "them cotton bolls got rotten," most of the sacks would be worn through on both sides. But they weren't through yet. The top two feet of the sack, which hadn't touched the ground, was cut off and made into hand towels. As far as we knew, they hadn't invented store-bought towels.

What did it take to make a good cotton picker? The usual answer was "a strong back and a weak mind." I guess I qualified on both counts. From a child, I learned the art and it was one thing I could excel at.

The old cotton patch. In spite of all the sore fingers, stickers, aching backs, and sore knees, I have never lost my love for farm life. If I were a few weeks younger, I would love to put on an old cotton sack and pull a few bolls. I'm sure the desire wouldn't last long but for a little time it would be fun.

Today, when I drive through cotton country and see those big machines harvesting cotton, I think of all our younger generation is missing by not having the experience of picking cotton.

But enough nostalgia for the moment. Back to the bottom land on the South Canadian River: The location was good for growing cotton, but not for staying healthy. This was mosquito-infested country (they bred in the river), so most of us were sick with malaria fever. I still remember the fever, the vomiting, and the taste of quinine—the only remedy at the time. We only stayed there a year.

5

GETTING AN EDUCATION—AT SCHOOL AND ELSEWHERE 1921

In 1921, Warren G. Harding was inaugurated as the 29th President of the United States. The first "Miss America" contest was held in Atlantic City. In Oklahoma, oil prices declined sharply, affecting the economy and the political climate.

EARLY DAY DOCTORING

Having mentioned malaria in the last chapter, a few words are in order regarding early day doctorin':

- Epsom salts, castor oil, and Black Draught were all guaranteed to cure constipation.

- Boric acid was a good eye wash.

- Whiskey was used to disinfect.

- Fat-meat poultices were put on boils.

- Baking soda was used as a cleaner, deodorant, and tooth powder. It was taken with water for sour stomach and heart burn. Baking-soda paste was spread on poison-oak rash.

- Vinegar was used as a hair rinse and to rinse the hands after washing the dishes with lye soap.

- The motto was "stuff a cold and starve a fever."

- Coal oil was one of man's greatest invention along with baling wire. It was the universal medicine, an all-around cure. One thing it was used for was bed bugs. Also, when your feet or other body parts were cut or punctured, you soaked the injured member in coal oil.

- Sulfur and grease was used for the seven-year itch. The seven-year itch was one of the most common ailments. It usually started in the fall and lasted all winter—until we took off our long-handle underwear. The remedy was to nightly rub the itching, burning, irritated skin with a mixture of sulfur and grease. You can imagine the odor of a school-room full of little bodies smeared with sulfur and grease.

  Speaking of odors, baths were taken weekly on Saturday nights—when possible—in a galvanized washtub. In the wintertime, it was placed as near the stove as possible (you weren't supposed to look). Regardless of the number of kids, only one tub full of water was used.

  Just thinking about it makes me start scratching and start smelling sulfur and grease. But it was all a part of life. No big deal. "Everybody was doin' it."

- Eventually, we had iodine and Milk of Magnesia.

The first of 1921, we moved back to the Stratford area—to Uncle Perry's place (Perry Rakestraw had married Dad's sister, Cecil Irene). Perry and Cecil had moved to Byars to live. Their forty-acre farm, which was located three miles northwest of Stratford, had a house on it. It was one of the nicest houses we ever lived in. It had three rooms and a back porch. The back porch had a dirt floor.

Frank Rakestraw and two daughters lived about an eighth of a mile down the hill.

While we lived at Uncle Perry's place, my great-uncle Andrew Roper came and stayed several weeks. He was Grandpa Hampy's brother and an old bachelor. He lived with his mother (my great-grandmother Roper) until she died and then he drifted from one family member to another. The story is told that one day Andrew thought W. M. had misbehaved and slapped him. That made Papa mighty unhappy and he told Andrew in no uncertain terms that it was not his job to discipline *his* children. Dad then said that, if Andrew was going to stay there, he should make himself helpful. He asked him to bring in a load of wood. Andrew, smarting from the reprimand from the younger man, went out the door and did not return. Did not return, that is, for six weeks. Six weeks later, he came back through the door—carrying a load of wood.

ONE-ROOM SCHOOL HOUSES

We walked about a mile to a two-room school called Cottonwood. They put me in the second grade. Janada was a beginner. They didn't worry much back then about what grade you should be in. They just asked, "Can you read, write, and cipher?" I remember the Elson Readers we used. Each day we read one page to the teacher. If we made no mistakes, we received a small gold star. It was pasted on the upper corner of that page. If we got five pages right in a row, we received a large gold star. How I worked for those stars!

I made my first public appearance in this school. An all-school program was produced on the theme of "America." I participated in a drill on the song "O Columbia, Gem of the Ocean." Grandma made me a costume consisting of a little red vest, a white shirt, and blue pants. Very patriotic. The school building had no stage, so the production was held on the porch using gas lights. Grandma kept that costume in her trunk for years.

A few comments on schools in rural Oklahoma at the time: The schools were generally one or two rooms. There was no air conditioning and heat came from a wood stove. Books and equipment were scarce. The three most common books were the Elson Reader, a speller, and an arithmetic book. We used Big Chief tablets and penny pencils made of cedar. Occasionally we used pens. They had removable points and were dipped in an ink well. But mainly we used pencils.

Few schools had a pencil sharpener. Each morning two boys were selected to sharpen the pencils. They gathered them up and went outside and sharpened them with their pocket knives. Can you imagine? Every boy had his own knife at school!

School lunches were whatever you could find at home (school lunches were not common for another twenty or so years): Maybe a cold biscuit with sausage or bacon. Maybe a jelly and butter sandwich. Maybe fruit when in season. Maybe some homemade cookies or molasses cake. Lunch was carried in a lard or syrup bucket, along with your own drinking cup. We usually had a large water bucket that everyone drank from.

Playground equipment was almost non-existent. Sometimes there was a home-made swing or see-saw, but mainly it was bring-your-own. For baseball, we had twine balls and home-made bats. The boys had tops to spin and marbles. Marbles were cheap and readily available. The most common kinds were peewees (small marbles made from clay), glassies, and agates. The last were extra special. Boys also played mumbly-peg, a game using pocket knives (not illegal in those days).

When I started to school, my favorite recess activity was riding a stick horse. I must have ridden a million miles and shot thousands of outlaws and Indians (sorry about that, Sam and W. M.). But, one day at recess, my horse turned too quickly and kicked a small girl. For some reason, they blamed *me* instead of my prancing, snorting steed!

The most exciting time at school was Friday afternoon when we chose up sides and had a ciphering match (arithmetic) or a spelling bee.

As you probably know, in those days switches were ready at hand and in common use by the teachers.

Walking home after school could be an adventure. At Cottonwood, there was a boy named Dan who liked to bully younger kids. My sister Hester finally got enough of Dan—and hit him over the head with her lunch bucket (a one-gallon lard bucket). That made a believer out of Dan. From that time on, he usually walked ahead or behind the rest of the crowd.

In May of 1921, shortly after school was out, Dad clipped all my hair off. (Dad gave me most of my haircuts until I was grown.) This was customary. This made your head cooler and also got your scalp clean after a winter of no washing. Soon after my annual clip, I came down with a fever which put me in bed for a few days. Grandma came and saw her favorite grandson sick in bed—without any hair. She was quick to voice her opinion: "My poor Son—sick, feverish, and no hair!" To her, this was an insult to the nth degree.

One day that summer, Janada and I decided we would play in the barn loft. We climbed up the ladder and were surprised and mystified at what we found: a brand new copper wash boiler. Why was it there and what was it for? We knew that boilers like that were generally used for boiling clothes, but we had an iron wash pot for that. And this boiler had never been used. We never mentioned the boiler to anyone else. Nor did we know until later that one use of these boilers was in making moonshine.

HOME-MADE WINE

In late August of '21, the possum grapes began to ripen. Dad and Oren sawed down a small tree that was covered with these grapes. They picked several bushels of them and put them in a fifty-gallon wooden barrel that sat on the porch. They took a wooden fence post and pounded the grapes until they were juicy. After adding lots of sugar, the barrel was covered with tow sacks and left to ferment for several days. (Any varmints that fell into this brew and drowned were just skimmed off.) Dad soon had his own special vintage of grape wine. When we went to town (or anywhere else), Dad would fill a gallon jug and put it under the spring seat of the wagon. The jug was always empty by the time it returned home. I don't remember Dad getting drunk on the wine, but it did make him talkative and happy-go-lucky.

We had very few acres to farm on the place. We raised cotton and corn mainly. Our cotton crop was early, and most of it was picked by October 1. I remember that the last of September, I went with Dad to sell a bale of cotton. It was cold and I was barefooted. I kept my feet warm by burying them in the soft, fluffy cotton. When the cotton was sold, Dad bought me my annual pair of shoes. That was always a thrilling thing: new shoes!

TERRIFIED!

Like most people, I have been frightened many times in my life, but one of the worst was while we were living at Uncle Perry's place. One day, I decided I would take a walk down through the field. When I had gone about half a mile, I heard a strange noise behind me. I turned and looked, and—lo and behold—about fifty yards away I saw a little man about two feet tall. He was waving his arms and emitting blood-curdling noises. One look was enough. I quickly made a large circle around him and headed full-speed for the house. All the time, I kept turning over in my mind who this was, what he wanted, and how dangerous he might be. I rushed into the house so breathless I could hardly talk: "Come quick. There is a little man down in the field!"

When my stepmother finally figured out what I was saying, she went with me, and we headed back to "the little man." When we got within about a hundred yards of the "man," she looked and said, "That's your little brother, W. M. He followed you to the field. He's crying because he couldn't catch you."

One of the events of 1921 was the purchase of a brand new yellow and green John Deere one-row riding lister planter. It was beautiful! To my remembrance, this was the one new implement my dad ever purchased.

MY FIRST GREAT JOURNEY

In early October, after our meager crops were gathered, my dad and Uncle Clyde (he was about 18 by this time) took me on the first Great Journey of my life. We traveled in our Model T to Mountain View, Oklahoma, to pick cotton—a distance of one hundred and fifty miles. The first night we were there, we slept in a corn crib, but the lady of the house couldn't stand to see a boy sleeping in the barn. The next day she moved Dad and me into one of her bedrooms and we ate with her family. While there, I celebrated my eighth birthday—in the cotton field.

This was Indian country (Kiowa). The Indians came to town on Saturdays, the women in large colored blankets and the men with long braided hair. Some of the locals delighted telling me terrifying Indian tales, and at that age, I believed them.

I picked cotton in a tow sack, and I'm sure I made a great hand. But after a week, Dad decided that I would be more valuable back on the farm. So, the day after my birthday, Uncle Clyde and I got on the train and started back. We couldn't make it in one day and had to spend the night in a hotel in Purcell, Oklahoma—a First for me. I was a world traveler!

HOME BUTCHERING—HOGS

I mentioned earlier that an annual ritual was the butchering of hogs. The last home butchering at our house was when I was eight years old—not long after the Mountain View trip—but it is still vivid in my memory. (If you are squeamish, you will want to skip this section.)

In the early days of the last century, every family in our corner of the world had the job of providing their own meat supply. Butcher shops were seldom found in small towns.

In early November, the hogs were fat enough to be slaughtered. Plus the weather was right for the annual ritual: Since we had no refrigeration, it had to be cold enough for the meat to keep. After a few frosty nights, Dad would decide the time was drawing near. He would start getting things ready for "the day":

- Supplies had to be purchased: salt, pepper, sausage seasoning, etc.
- Knives had to be sharpened.

- A pole axe or gun would be needed for the killing.
- There had to be a place to hang the carcasses.
- A barrel for scalding the hog was needed.
- The big iron wash pot was readied for heating the water.
- There had to be a wooden platform in front of the barrel for laying the hog on while it was being scraped.
- Wood for the fire had to be cut.
- Lots of wash tubs and buckets were needed for holding the meat scraps (fat and sausage trimmings) and waste products.

The day before the event, all the equipment and supplies were put into place. The hogs were put in a small pen. The wash pot was filled with water. Wood was put beneath the pot, ready to be lit. After supper, Dad would say, "Bedtime! We've got a big day tomorrow." The day was a fun day for us kids, but work for the oldies. But since there were always relatives or neighbors helping, I guess it was a time of fellowship even for them.

We were up at the crack of dawn. Breakfast was quickly prepared and eaten. Dad would go out, light the fire under the wash pot, give the hogs a little feed to keep them quiet, and then roll a RJR cigarette and sit quietly by the wood stove waiting for the neighbors to arrive. About 8:30, two families came, bringing two kids about my age.

The men visited briefly. The women went into the house to see what needed to be done. After a final inspection of all facilities and equipment, the men headed for the hog pen. Dad took his sticking knife and another man took the pole axe. The hogs were crowded into a corner. Two men grabbed one of them and held him while a third man hit him between the eyes with the blunt side of the axe head. He fell. Quick as a flash, Dad straddled the hog, turned him on his back and deftly cut his throat.

In a few minutes, the hog was ready to be taken to the scalding barrel, which had been filled with water from the wash pot. Two men dragged the pig the short distance to the barrel. The water was tested for temperature. Too cold and the hair wouldn't come off. Too hot, the hair would set and not come off. One man dipped his finger three times into the water. If it burned on the third dip, it was right.

Two men got hold of the back legs of the hog and stuffed him headfirst into the barrel. They plunged him up and down three or four times, then tested to see if the bristles were loose. If not, they repeated the process. When they determined the bristles were loose, they dragged him out, switched ends, and repeated the process.

Finally the carcass was pulled out and laid on a makeshift platform in front of the barrel. Everybody that could get around him would grab a knife and start scraping. Bristles would fly. After twenty to thirty minutes the scraping was done and the hog ready to hang up. To hang it up, the tendons of the back legs were cut and a single tree inserted in them.

Hot water was poured over the hog and he was thoroughly cleaned. Then the carcass was cut down the midline of the belly—clear down to the throat. The internal organs were carefully cut loose and taken out and put in a tub. This gutting was done by the most experienced butcher present. The women were waiting. They removed the heart and liver and stripped the fat from the intestines.

The inside of the cavity was lined with layers of fat. This was called leaf lard. This was pulled loose and put in the lard container. Along the backbone was the tenderloin, the best of all meat. This was cut out and usually was cooked that day, along with biscuits and gravy. Yum! The ribs were taken out and the carcass thoroughly washed inside. The head was removed and the carcass hung up to chill during the night. One pig down and two more to go.

While the first hog was being cleaned and dressed, other men had been working on the second. The same procedure was followed. By lunch time, the second hog was hung. The women, who had been busy stripping fat and trimming out parts for sausage, had stopped to prepare the tenderloin for lunch.

After a good lunch and a bit of rest, the men went back to finish off the third hog. About 4:00 o'clock, the last one was hung and the neighbors prepared to leave. They took some ribs, liver, and tenderloin for their work. Dad and the rest of the family had the job of cleaning up and getting ready for what had to be done the next day.

The next morning, Dad laid a chilled carcass on an improvised table outside and began the process of preparing the meat for curing and storage. First the backbone was cut out, dividing the hog into two parts. The backbone was always eaten fresh; it was delicious either boiled or roasted. Then each of the two halves were divided into three parts: the ham, the shoulder, and bacon. All of these were carefully trimmed of excess fat. The feet were cut off and set aside for pickling.

Then Dad started on the head. After more cleaning, the skull was opened and the brains extracted. These were usually fried with eggs for a breakfast delicacy. The jowls were removed and salted down.

After all this was done, some boiled the head and used the bits of meat to make "hogshead souce": They pressed the bits of meat together until it make a kind of loaf which they would slice and eat (poor folks' lunchmeat). Some cut the intestines into narrow strips and dropped them into hot deep fat to make chitterlings (better known as "chitlins"). Also the intestines were sometimes used as the casing for the sausage.

After Dad finished the trimming, the pieces were thoroughly washed and hung up to dry overnight. The next morning, the meat box was readied and salting down began. Each piece was covered with plain stock salt, which was gently rubbed in. Then the meat was placed in the box. Most farms had a smoke house where the meat was smoked and stored throughout the year, but we never smoked our meat. After a few weeks in the salt box, the meat was hung up. Dad's butchering job was done for the year except for putting everything away.

But the women still had work to do. They made sausage from the bits and pieces of lean meat. The fat trimmings were put in the big black wash pot outside and cooked until the fat was liquid. It was then drained off and put in one-or five-gallon lard buckets. The cracklings that remained in the pot were saved for eating and cooking. Cracklin' cornbread was always a treat. After the lard and eatable cracklings were removed, there was always "stuff" left. This was used for the women's last job: making lye soap. Folks found a use for everything but the squeal.

As I said, I was eight years old the last time our family had a home butchering, but I did a lot of it after I became a vocational-agriculture teacher and helped farmers. My last attempt was twenty years ago at Pernell, Oklahoma. This bloody, smelly, back-breaking ritual is one feature of "the good old days" I can live without!

"MY KIDS, YOUR KIDS, AND OUR KIDS"

On December 22, 1921, my half-brother Hansel J. "Hank" Roper was born. I now had sisters, step-brothers, and a half-brother. Thus the joke started of Dad running into the house and shouting to Oren, *"My* kids and *your* kids are beatin' the stuffin's out of *our* kids!"*

At the end of the year, we moved back to the Old Home Place, about two miles away.

6

AN OLD HOUSE, RELIGION, AND MOONSHINE
1922

*1922 saw the beginning of the **Reader's Digest**, the helicopter, and the first radio commercial. The same year, the "Teapot Dome" scandal discredited Harding's administration. In Oklahoma, John C. Watson campaigned for governor, using a jazz band to collect a crowd and arouse enthusiasm. He was elected in November.*

When I was eight, my father decided to move back to the one and only piece of ground he ever "owned": a forty-acre tract on which he was making payments. He had lived there a few years after he married my mother. The place was located two and one-half miles northeast of McGee School, near Stratford, Oklahoma. The land joined Grandpa Hampy's fifty acres. The improvements consisted of one dilapidated two-room house that had not been lived in for several years.

SETTING UP HOUSE

The process of renovating the house began with covering the inside walls with cardboard boxes. (Sheetrock wasn't available in those days.) After that, old newspapers were pasted on the wall with flour paste—making an interesting conversation piece (when you were bored, you could read the wall). The floors were thoroughly scrubbed with lye water and rat holes were covered with small pieces of tin. Broken window panes were covered with cardboard, and cracks around window sills were chinked with scraps of cloth. Window curtains or shades were not considered needful or necessary. There were no pictures on the wall and no floor coverings. Cracks in the floor allowed water to drain.

The roof leaked in several places. Pans were put under the leaks to catch the water when it rained.

The furnishings of the house were the necessary items common to most country homes: In the kitchen was the kitchen stove (wood-burning), a table (home-made), two or three old wooden chairs, a few wooden boxes, and a long wooden bench on one side of the table for the kids. The table was covered with an oil cloth, and in the center of the table sat a kerosene lamp. Orange crates or apple boxes were nailed on the wall for cabinets. The few pots and pans we owned hung on nails on the wall above the stove.

Our towels were made from worn-out cotton sacks after the cotton season was over. Our tea towels and strainer cloths were made from flour sacks.

On one side of the kitchen, we had an old wooden box that served as a wash stand. On it was a zinc bucket filled with water. Sometimes we had a good dipper, and sometimes a tin cup served as dipper. The wash pan was usually tin, but a granite-ware wash pan could be purchased. The wash stand was usually near the door so used water could be thrown out into the yard. You didn't go to bed with the water bucket empty.

We also had a wood box in the kitchen. Every evening, it was the kids' job to see that kindling was brought in and that the wood box was filled.

An iron bedstead was also in the kitchen, up against the wall. It had springs and a corn-shuck mattress for summer. If you were prosperous, you had a feather bed for winter. My three sisters slept in the kitchen.

The other room was the bedroom. It had a wood-burning heating stove. That old stove was always either too hot or too cold. It was always needing wood or the ashes needed to be cleaned out.

Clothes closets were unnecessary because we had very few extra clothes other than a few "good clothes" that needed starching and ironing. If needed, baling wire was stretched across one corner of the room and an old sheet or blanket curtain was put up (baling wire was one of man's great inventions; you could fix 'most anything with baling wire). Clothes were hung on nails driven in the wall (clothes hangers were not part of our life). Extra quilts or blankets were kept in a trunk, which was also used for a chair.

This room had one double-bed, which served as the sleeping quarters for Dad and Mom—and small children. Most always one child slept in the middle of the bed, and, when needed, another child slept at the foot of the bed. (My heart bleeds for the modern child who doesn't have his own room.) Usually we had a half bed in a corner of the room, the bed for the two boys. At any given time, at least one of those boys had a bed-wetting problem—but we won't talk about that.

At this time, there were "only" six of us kids at home.

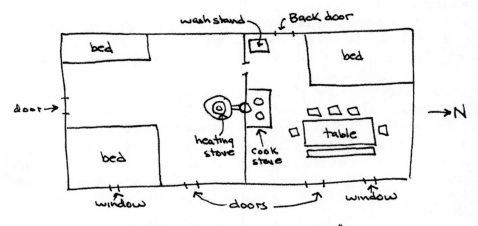

HOUSE ON "OLD HOME PLACE"

After the house was livable, we needed a hen house. A neighbor had an old log corn crib, about 12' x 12' in size. He said we could have it if we wanted to move it. We took it down log by log, moved it, and set it back up. We used it for a few Dominiquer hens.

For crops, we had cotton, some corn, a half acre of sorghum, and about an acre of sweet potatoes. We also planted some fruit trees. I was only a tad, but being the oldest boy, I got the privilege of plowing with a one-row walking cultivator. The fields were grassy (crabgrass) and had lots of stumps. The stumps had to be hoed around, which took lots of time. The Lord said men would have "thorns" and "thistles"; I guess He forgot to mention the stumps!

THE OLD SORGHUM MILL

In late August, we stripped and cut the sorghum cane and hauled it to the sorghum mill where it was made into molasses, the standard sweetener for country folks.

Most of the year, the sorghum mill—which belonged to a neighbor—sat lonely on the side of a hill near the bank of Big Creek. In the mind of a child, that pile of machinery was one of the greatest inventions of our time—next to baling wire and the marvelous machine which had recently come into being ("the horse-less carriage," the Model T by Henry Ford).

Each year we planted about a half acre of Blue Ribbon cane for the special purpose of making sorghum 'lasses. In late August or early September, the cane ripened—making a stalk about eight feet tall with a reddish-brown seed head. In harvesting, a wooden knife about two feet long and four inches wide—beveled on one side—was used to strip the leaves from the stalk. Then a large corn knife or machete was used to cut the stalk down. The stalks were laid in piles along the row. The younger set came along and hacked off the heads with a butcher knife. From there, the stalks were hauled in a wagon to the mill.

The molasses-making process had two parts: First, the juice had to be extracted. This was done by running the stalks through two huge iron wheels (presses). A team of horses was hooked to a long overhead beam and driven around and around, turning the presses. One man had the job running the stalks through the press. The juice was strained through a tow sack to remove a part of the debris and was caught in a fifty-gallon wooden barrel.

Second, the juice had to be cooked in a cooking pan or vat. Grandpa Roper was in charge of changing the raw juice into molasses. The pan he used was set under a large tree about seventy five yards downhill from the press—so the juice would flow down to it. The cooking pan was set on a foundation about three feet high and was made of steel. It was about twelve feet long, four feet wide, and about twelve inches high—and had several partitions.

A wood fire was started early in the morning under the vat. By the time the juice was squeezed, the pan was hot enough to receive it. A spigot was opened in the barrel, juice ran down a pipe to the vat, and the cooking process began. Two men with skimmers walked along the side of the pan removing the scum that came to the top as the juice cooked.

The juice came into the vat at the top end. As it cooked, it was moved through the partitions until it reached the lower end. When done (the Molasses Maker knew when it was ready), the molasses was drained into new gallon buckets with lids and was ready for eating or selling. Usually the owner of the mill received a portion of the syrup instead of money.

As a young'un, I enjoyed driving the horses around and around, chewing on sweet stalks of cane, and sampling the new-made 'lasses. I'm sure the men didn't like it as well; it was a hot sweaty job. But we got a supply of molasses for the year—and, after all, the molasses-making season didn't last long.

As a lad, the sweetest and greatest smell that came to my tender nostrils was the odor of Grandma's fresh-from-the-oven molasses cake. We used little sugar—it cost money and that was a scarce item—so for sweetener, it was sorghum molasses. The molasses sat in middle of the table in a special aluminum pitcher year round. In winter, when it became cold, the molasses would get so thick that it wouldn't pour. Thus an expression was invented for anyone who moved slowly: "Slower than molasses in the winter."

A NEW POTATO HOUSE!

In early October 1922, the sweet potatoes were ready to harvest. The sandy soil of the old home place was a natural for growing sweet potatoes, but to grow sweet potatoes for market, they had to be cured. So during the month of August, Dad, with the help from a neighbor, built the only new structure he ever built in his life. (He lived 74 years and never even built a new outhouse; the only new structure was a potato house.)

From a local sawmill, Dad bought (on credit) rough-sawed oak lumber, enough to build a house 12' x 18'. It was double-walled. When the walls were finished, they were filled with clay soil for insulation. Bins were built on each side, with a hall down the middle. The attic was also filled with clay and was topped with a sheet-iron roof. There was one door, no windows. A wood-burning stove stood in place in the middle of the house, ready for firing. It was a magnificent structure! Our own new potato house!

The sweet potatoes were dug with a one-row lister and then picked up by hand and placed in a bushel basket. They were hauled to the potato house where they were stored in bins for curing. The wood stove in the middle of the house was kept burning around the clock for two or three weeks, keeping the temperature right for the drying-out process. About the first of November, an uncle came by on horse back and told Dad that a company was buying enough sweet potatoes to fill a railroad car at Byars, Oklahoma (about twelve miles away). He was giving a dollar per bushel. This was a good price, so in great excitement, a wagon was loaded and we went on a day's travel to market!

During the spring semester of the 1921-22 school year, we walked two and a half miles to the McGee School. While I was growing up, as a rule, I had to work in the fall and only got to go to school during the spring semester.

SMOKING AND TOBACCO

About this time, I tried smoking for the first time. The other boys and I would hide behind the barn and smoke corn silks. Sometimes, we would cut lengths from a dried grape vine and smoke them. Those vines could knock your head off!

The sickest I remember being was during a Pentecostal meeting. These meetings were informal: People were always coming and going, and nobody paid much attention to what the children were doing. While the adults were inside, trying to get saved, one of the kids came up with a package of Beech Nut chewing tobacco. I took a BIG bite and started chewing. The only time I remember being sicker was when I had a gallbladder attack sixty years later.

OLD TIME RELIGION

Speaking of Pentecostal meetings, this is a good a time to tell you about religion in my part of the world. Religion in my life up to age 7 or 8 was practically non-existent. We lived in the country with few churches around. I have no memory of prayers, Bible reading, or religious teaching at our house. The only time "grace" was said at our house was when Grandma visited.

But we sometimes lived with my Grandma Roper, who was very religious. Every year, about August after the crops had been laid by, there would be a revival meeting somewhere not too far off. Grandma was not selective about attending revivals. When one was in town, we attended.

Grandpa would hook up the horses, and we'd all pile into the wagon and off we'd go. The kids would sit in the wagon bed on old cotton sacks or old quilts. Later in the evening, those same coverings would be spread on the ground as pallets for the kids to sleep on.

These meetings were often held under brush arbors. The seating consisted of 2 x 12s laid on blocks of wood. Those who had troubles with hard seats brought quilts to sit on. Between the seats and around the arbor, on the ground, would be dozens of pallets for sleeping children.

Most of the arbor meetings were conducted by Holiness preachers, sometimes referred to as "holy rollers." Some of the more energetic and enthusiastic preachers were women. What these men and women lacked in Biblical knowledge, they made up for in stamina. They preached life short, death certain, eternity long, and hell hot—and they preached it long and loud.

Singing would take about an hour at the beginning of the service. The singing was loud and jubilant, usually accompanied by a pump organ and maybe a guitar or banjo. A favorite song was "When the Saints Go Marching In." Others were "There's Power in the Blood" and "Revive Us Again."

There was a large lady at a meeting one night who had an unusually loud voice. After the meeting, Grandma went up to her and said, "If I had a trumpet like yours, I'd toot it all the time."

Following the singing would be the "testimony service." This was spontaneous. Folks would pop up off their wooden seats and tell what the Lord had done with them and for them. In general, these speeches would last from three to fifteen minutes. The longer they lasted, the more emotional they would become. The "hallelujahs" and "amens" echoed through the night. Many times two or three would talk at the same time. If it was a good "popcorn" meeting (with people popping up and down), arms would begin to wave and bodies would begin to sway. Some might begin to "speak in tongues." As "the Spirit took hold," folks might begin to fall in the floor or start running about. In the mind of a small child, this was exciting.

By this time, the audience was warmed to a fever pitch and it was time for the preacher to start his (or her) sermon. I still remember some of the fiery sermons I heard when I was a boy. The texts were often from the Book of Revelation, and the lessons would be on "the mark of the beast," the Second Coming, the Judgment and the like. There were no fifteen-or twenty-minute homilies, but two hours of fire and brimstone. They were enough to scare you into heaven—or at least make you want to stay out of hell.

After the sermon, there would be thirty to sixty minutes of "altar call" and prayers for the backsliders and reprobates. There was always an "altar" at the front of the building where those seeking help could come and pray. Usually this was a wooden bench across the front of the meeting place. During the singing of the invitation songs (there were generally several), faithful members would go into the audience to friends and family and get on their knees and tearfully implore their loved ones to be saved.

The prayers at the altar would begin. They were loud and persistent, beseeching the Lord to save the poor sinful soul from the fiery furnace of hell. Usually other friends would join in the prayers for the sinner. But not all at the altar were seeking salvation. Some were seeking "sanctification—a second blessing." Others were begging the Lord to baptize them in the Holy Ghost.

Sometimes a person would jump up saying, "I got it!" They would bounce up and down, thanking the Lord. If they thought they got the Holy Spirit, they would start "speaking in tongues."

After three or four hours, the meeting would wind down. The prayers came to an end and a final song was sung. The wagons were loaded with sleeping kids and the journey home began. We arrived home about midnight or 1:00 a.m., tired and worn out but happy in the thought "We've been to a revival!"

MOONSHINING IN OKLAHOMA

Moving from the Spirit to spirits: About this time, I became aware of the moonshine activities of the area. One day, my sisters and I were walking in the woods close to our house—across the fence on someone else's property. Near a spring, we came across a buried fifty-gallon barrel that looked like someone had taken an axe to it. It was what remained of a moonshine operation.

Once Clifford Biles and I (a couple of nine-year-old buddies) rode in a wagon with Papa and Glen Biles to a spot some distance away. Papa and Glen left us to play with some other children while they went off into the woods with some other men. It was generally understood, though not mentioned, that the men had gone to a still. Late that night, they came back and picked us up and took us home.

There were a couple of revenuers who lived in Stratford that spent all their time looking for stills. Once they came to our house and took Dad to town. After threatening him, they turned him loose. I'm not sure that my father ever had a still—though the destroyed mash barrel we found may have been his. Mainly he just liked to drink with his buddies.

But others in the family definitely took an active part in the production of moonshine. One was my uncle, Clayton B. Roper. I remember at least three locations where Clayton had moonshine operations.

Once, revenuers came to Clayton's house looking for buried mash barrels. The two men had wagon rods and they walked around the yard poking in the dirt, trying to discover where the barrels were. What they didn't know was that the mash barrel was in a back room of the house. Clayton's friends would stand on the front porch for a while watching the government men and then they would go in the back room and take a drink. Then they would go back to the porch. As time went by, the men on the porch were feeling no pain and began taunting the revenuers: "Have you checked over by the barn?" "Hey, I betcha it's over by the well!" The inspectors came up dry that time (no pun intended).

On another occasion, someone shouted, "The revenuers are coming!" One of Clayton's buddies jumped on a horse, grabbed up an empty fifty-gallon barrel, and rode off into the woods. I suppose he figured the barrel would be considered incriminating evidence.

Once Clayton was arrested because of incriminating evidence—a 100-pound bag of sugar—and spent some time in jail. Sugar was put up in 100-pound bags, but even in those days when cooking was from scratch, few (other than moonshiners) bought sugar in such quantities. Grandma Ada was incensed. As far as she was concerned, her boys could do no wrong. "They arrested poor Clayton just because he bought sugar in a 100-pound bag," she protested. "Why Clayton has *always* bought his sugar in 100-pound bags."

"MISSED IT BY *THAT* MUCH!"

During 1922, while we were living on the old home place, we had our one chance to "get rich": The oil business was still booming and a man came by and offered Dad $1,000.00 to lease the mineral rights on his property. $1,000.00! That was more money than any of us had ever seen at one time! That was ten bales of cotton, twenty or twenty-five head of cattle! But before the man could carry through on the deal, he was killed in an accident. Our dream of being the oil-rich Stratford Hillbillies died almost as soon as it was born.

By the time the fall of 1922 had rolled around, Grandpa Hampy and Grandma Ada had decided to quit farming and had built themselves a three-room home in Stratford. Dad rented their place (it joined ours). It had about fifty acres and a three-room house with a small porch. We were getting up in the world: farming two farms and living in a big house. We even had a good barn. But then Grandma decided that my sisters and I had too far to walk to school, so she insisted that we come live with them in Stratford. For a change, we went to school both semesters that school year.

7

GRANDMA'S HOUSE—AND MOVING ON MY BIRTHDAY 1923

In 1923, Harding died and Calvin Coolidge became president. As prohibition was enforced, "speak-easies" flourished, and the Charleston became the dance craze. In Oklahoma, John C. Watson, the fifth governor, placed the state under martial law because of the terrorist activities of the Ku Klux Klan which had become a political force in the state. Watson's days in office were "few and full of trouble." He was impeached after only nine months in office, and the lieutenant governor Martin E. Trapp became the sixth governor of Oklahoma.

A Joke That Backfired

The first part of 1923, I was nine, living with my grandparents in Stratford and attending school there. The school building was heated with steam heat. One cold and frosty March morning, as we arrived at school, we were informed that we would have to go home because the furnace was not working.

As I neared home, a Great Thought came into my mind. I started whimpering and crying as I walked into the room where Grandma was at one of her usual jobs: scrubbing clothes on a rub board.

Grandma quickly asked, "Why are you crying?"

"They expelled me from school."

Did you ever see a Grandma explode? She jerked off her apron, grabbed her coat with one hand and me with the other, and out the door we flew.

I was scared and almost speechless. I could barely make out what she was saying: "They can whip you, but they are not going to keep you from going to school!"

I opened my mouth and started to explain, but Grandma was too "het up" to listen. "I'll show them what they can do!" she said.

Finally, about half way to the school house, Grandma got winded, and she listened to what I had to say.

I did not try that again.

GRANDMA'S HOUSE

In those days, there was no government welfare, Social Security, or food stamps. You worked or you went hungry. After my grandparents moved off the farm, Grandma made most of the living by taking in washing (using the rub board) and ironing for other people. In her spare time she did quilting. She always had a quilt in the frame—which hung down from the ceiling. She received $1.50 per spool of thread used. Most quilts used one spool. She was careful with her money. She and Grandpa never had much, but she was never broke. When an emergency arose, she always found the money to take care of it.

Among other responsibilities, Grandma was the provider and care-taker of the bedding. She raised geese and plucked their feathers to fill pillows and mattresses. Feather bedding made for warm sleeping in the winter time. In the summer, we slept on mattress stuffed with corn shucks as they were cooler sleeping. My grandparents may have been poor in many ways, but there were a few possessions Grandma was proud of. One was her bed. When she got up in the morning, she made the bed with the fanciest bed spread and best pillows she had. That bed stayed that way all day long. No one—not even I—was allowed to sit on it.

GRANDMA'S RELIGION

I have mentioned that Grandma was very religious. She tried hard to "let her light shine," to live a godly life. I can still hear her singing as she went about her work. Some of her favorite songs were "The Lily of the Valley," "In the Sweet By and By," and "The Old Rugged Cross." Grandma always asked the blessing before each meal. She continually taught us kids about God.

Her religion influenced the way she looked at life. Grandpa came in one morning from feeding the horses, and said, "Ol' Shorty's dead." Grandma said, with enthusiasm, "Well, thank the Lord!" Grandpa exploded. "Why did you say that?!" Grandma said, "I'm thankful that ol' Dan is still living!" (Ol' Dan was their other horse.)

Grandma was faithful in attendance at the Missionary Baptist Church. She saw to it that we went to Sunday School and church. On Sunday evening before the worship service, the young people had a meeting called B.Y.P.U. (Baptist Young People's Union) which we attended and enjoyed.

Grandma firmly believed that the Lord wanted neat and clean worshippers. When we lived with her, we always had our Saturday night bath (in a no. 3 wash-tub). On Sunday, our hair was always cleaned and combed, our shoes shined, and we had our best clothes on. They may have been patched, but they were washed and ironed. Grandma always had a Sunday dress, a pair of white gloves, and a hat. If the Lord came on Sunday, she wanted to meet Him in her best.

As I've mentioned before, Grandpa was not a church-goer. There were a few times I remember him taking the rest of us to church, but I don't remember seeing him in a church building.

One Easter, Grandma wanted everyone in church. Grandma got up early to get everyone ready. She put on her best dress and her hat and gloves. Then she got the girls ready. While she was doing that, Grandpa came into the house hunting his fish hooks. He went outside and starting digging for worms. He saw me watching him and asked me if I would like to go fishing with him. The day was warm and beautiful. To a youngster who seldom got to fish, this was an invitation hard to turn down. I asked Grandma about it. "The Lord would like to see you at church," she said, "but it's your choice." I went with Grandpa.

We took off for the fishing hole. We walked across fields and pastures—about a mile I guess—until we reached a small creek. Grandpa cut some willow poles, tied the fishing lines on the poles, and baited the hooks with wiggling red worms. The water couldn't have been more than two feet deep.

We fished in all the nooks and crannies of the little creek until about five o'clock and started for home. I was carrying three small perch, strutting like a peacock, proud beyond measure of my success as a fisherman. Without a word of reproach, Grandma cleaned and cooked those three little fish. But I still had a guilty feeling for "breaking the Sabbath" (as Grandma would say) that Easter Sunday.

We stayed with Grandpa and Grandma until the school was out in May. Then we went back to Papa's farm to work during the summer. Dad made good crops that year: cotton plus corn, cane, and kafir for the animals.

THE DEATH OF THE FAMILY MOONSHINER

During the summer of 1923, Uncle Clayton died under suspicious circumstances. It was rumored that Clayton's wife, Josephine, had a boyfriend named Chisholm. Clayton confronted her with the rumor. Not long after that, Clayton came down with a horrendous belly-ache. I remember riding in the car with Clayton to the hospital at Ada, and Clayton saying, "I'm not going to get much sleep with this!" He passed away August 10, 1923. According to funeral home records, he died of "a bowel problem." Grandma Ada was always convinced that Josephine and the alleged boyfriend gave Clayton poisoned moonshine.

Josephine and her alleged boyfriend married soon after.

MOVING ON MY BIRTHDAY

When school started in the fall, we moved back to our grandparents' home and I started the fifth grade.

It had been a good year for our family, but Dad couldn't stand prosperity. He had seen the good lands of western Oklahoma. So, when I was almost ten, my father decided to sell out and move to Mountain View, Oklahoma. About all he had to sell was his corn crop. He suspended a 50-gallon barrel from a scale in the barn. When someone wanted to buy some corn, they would weigh the corn in the barrel and then dump it in the buyer's wagon. We kept a few chickens and one old milk cow for the move.

On Sunday, October 5, 1923, my tenth birthday, neighbors came and helped us load two wagons. We left about 1:30 p.m., Papa driving one wagon and me the other. We made it to Byars, about ten miles, before we stopped for the night. We spent the night with Uncle Perry and Aunt Cecil (Roper) Rakestraw.

The next day, as we traveled westward, a car hit our cow, but the cow didn't seem to be hurt much. We made it to Purcell, and spent the night at a wagon yard—a cross between a stable and a motel. For 50¢, you got to drive your wagon under a shed and then you had a room in which you could cook your evening meal. This was our only night at a wagon yard.

The following day, we made it to Tabler, about eight miles east of Chickasha. We spent the night at a campground. I forget all the stops, but I remember camping near Verdan. We would camp by the side of the road and sleep in the wagon. During the daytime, we kids would often walk and play alongside the wagon as it rolled along. Altogether it took seven days to make a one hundred and fifty mile trip.

Our destination was a farm three miles north of Mountain View. Dad had made arrangements to pick cotton for a farmer named Neil. Cotton was good that year and we picked for him all fall. After breakfast, we would head for the field. Oren would clean the house, then fix our lunch (which always included a can or two of pork and beans) and bring it to the field. We would take about thirty minutes to eat and start down the rows again. When our sacks were full, we got a short break while Dad weighed them and dumped the cotton in the wagon. Dad got no break but he didn't complain.

We lived in a two-room tar-paper shack, close to the farmer's house. We cooked on a monkey stove. A monkey stove was a small, squat, cooking stove with a square flat top. There was no oven in the stove itself, but some of the models had a small oven fitted about half-way up the stovepipe that came out of the stove. The oven utilized the heat coming up the stovepipe. The stove used by our family had this deluxe feature. The shack we lived in was just a few hundred yards north of Oakdale school, but we got no schooling that fall.

Near the close of the year, we rented a place from "Grandpa" Pewther (most old people were called "Grandpa" and "Grandma"), two miles north and one mile west of Mountain View. December 23, 1923, Troy Lee was born, my second half-brother.

8

GOING UNDER THE THIRD TIME 1924

In 1924, J. Edgar Hoover became the head of the FBI, and Calvin Coolidge was re-elected by a landslide. In Oklahoma, Gov. Trapp started construction of all-weather roads throughout the state.

The winter of 23–24 was cold and hard. We cut fish frozen from the ice. We had no milk cow. Grandpa Pewther, who lived about a half mile away, gave us a gallon of skim milk each day. I drank skim milk and ate oatmeal long before it was "cool."

We children started to the Oakdale school in January, 1924. Oakdale, a two-room country school, was about two miles from our home. I was in the fifth grade.

The principal sports at Oakdale were marbles and tops. We used the tops in a manner similar to marbles: We saved tags from chewing tobacco. Those tags were put in a circle drawn on the ground. If your spinning top knocked a tag from the circle, it was yours (as in "keeps" in marbles). We also occasionally pitched pennies.

A LITTLE RELIGION NEVER HURT ANYONE

I have indicated that religion was not a priority in our household. Except when Grandma visited, we had no prayers. We had no religious discussion. We had no religious materials other than a Bible which sat, unread, in whatever room served as our living room.

But, during the two years we were at Mountain View, in addition to the summer revival meetings, we occasionally visited a Pentecostal church. Oren's mother had been a member of that church. Oren probably considered herself a member although I do not remember her taking a part in the public worship service.

We had one other minor religious influence: Back in those days, everyone went to town on Saturday. Sometimes itinerate preachers came through and preached on the street corners on Saturdays. They generally drew a good crowd with subjects such as "God Made Everything But a Mule."

GOING UNDER THE THIRD TIME

The summer of 1924, after school was out, I nearly drowned in Pewther's lake. This was a big farm pond, but "Pewther's lake" was what it was called. We would sneak off to swim there and generally fool around. One attraction was a small home-made boat about six–eight feet long that was kept tied to the bank. It leaked, but was still fun to play in.

One day, when we arrived, the boat had gotten loose and was floating in the middle of the lake. It was sitting low in the water. It had obviously leaked quite a bit. But we wanted to play with it. I was one of the older boys (I was ten), and was convinced that I was one of the best swimmers. I said, "I'll go get it." I knew it wouldn't be easy, but I figured I could make it as far as the boat. Then I could crawl on the boat and hand paddle it back to the bank.

By the time I made it to the boat, I was exhausted but was feeling pretty good about being able to get there. I reached out and grabbed the boat. The boat, which was filled with water, instantly—glub, glub—sank. I panicked. I glanced at both banks, decided the opposite shore looked a little closer, and started for it.

I struggled until I got within about twenty feet of the bank. My fatigued brain thought "I'm within twenty feet. I can probably touch bottom." I put my feet down. No bottom. I sank. Spluttering, I struggled to the surface, stroked my arms four or five more times—and tried again. I sank again. Panic-stricken, I made it back to the surface and splashed forward another few feet—and tried once more. I went down for the third time.

When I got my head above water, I was only ten or so feet from the bank, but I knew I was doomed. I had always heard, "If you go down three times, you drown." After a few more splashes, my feet finally touched bottom and I struggled onto the bank. I stood on my head in an effort to get all the water out.

Though I was now on the bank, I was still convinced that I would drown at any moment. After all, I had gone down three times!

HOW TO MAKE REAL COFFEE

I started drinking coffee about this time. Coffee for breakfast was a necessity in our house. We always drank Peaberry coffee, which came in bean form in a brown paper bag and had to be ground. We used a pound of Peaberry every week.

Dad made the coffee in a large gray granite coffee pot. In the past, it had probably been new and shiny. But I remember it as old and blackened with years of use. The granite was chipped in places, the lid hanging on with baling wire. Sitting on the back of the stove, it was always ready for the brewing of that age-old stimulant.

An hour or so before dawn, I would hear one or two old roosters crow and, shortly after, the sound of the coffee grinder. I usually turned over and went back to sleep, secure in the thought that Dad had things under control and all was well with the world.

For years, Dad had an unerring routine: He would get up around 4:00 a.m., build fires in the wood stoves, fill the teakettle with water and put it on the stove to heat. It was then time to get down the coffee grinder. He poured in a cup of Peaberry coffee beans and ground them. He put the grounds into the coffee pot, along with a few cups of water. (He figured that it didn't take much water to make a cup of coffee.) Then the pot was set on the stove.

Dad "built" his elixir. After breakfast each Saturday, the pot was emptied and washed. On Sunday morning, a cup of ground coffee was put in the pot, water added, and the pot put on the stove to boil. After breakfast, the pot was pushed to the back of the stove, where it sat until the next morning. At that time, another cup of fresh grounds was added, along with water. So it went through the week. After boiling for a week, by Saturday morning the draught was thick enough for a spoon to stand upright. (Someone started the rumor that the spoon *dissolved* in Dad's favorite drink—an obvious exaggeration.)

None of the kids were forbidden to drink the stuff, but I was one of the few who did. Dad's idea of "building" a cup of coffee has stayed with me. I've used a modified version for years—much to the chagrin of my daughters-in-law who use electric "coffee makers." Oh well, a few added spoons of instant coffee can make manufactured coffee drinkable.

9

TRYING TO STAY OUT OF TROUBLE 1925

In 1925, Al Capone took control of Chicago's bootlegging racket. Babe Ruth received the unheard-of salary of $52,000 for the year. In Oklahoma, the gasoline tax was increased to three cents a gallon.

When January 1925 rolled around, we were still living in Pewther's house north of Mountain View. We kids continued to attend at the Oakdale school. We stayed two years in that house. Two years in the same place! For a Roper, that was growing deep roots!

PLAYING HOOKY

I recall one of my earlier sins from my Oakdale days: The Washita River had flooded, creating little "lakes" all over the bottom land. Fish from the river were trapped in these bodies of water, a lot of fish. An eighth-grade neighbor boy and I decided that those fish needed to be caught. One of us went to the teacher and said, "I'm sick." Later, the other one told the teacher the same sad tale. We met a quarter of a mile away, over the hill. We rigged up some kind of seine and caught a string of catfish. They weren't big, but there were a lot of them. If there were repercussions from this transgression, I don't remember them.

Our closest neighbor was Lander McManus. Lander was an old hunter and fisherman, a Mountain Man without a mountain. He knew how to make nets out of twine. He made them in his spare time and sold them. One net he made was a hoop net. This was a cone-shaped net with a mouth two–three feet in diameter. It stretched out ten to twelve feet to a point.

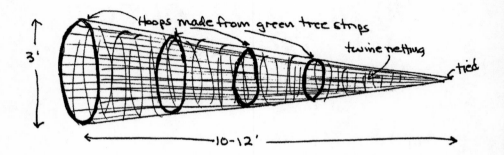

In use, it was anchored underwater in the river with the mouth pointing downstream. Fish would swim into it and then they couldn't get out. We chopped cotton for him several days and he made us one. ("Chopping cotton" = using a hoe to chop weeds out of the rows of young cotton plants.) We had fish all summer.

WALKING IN MY SLEEP

Occasionally, I walked in my sleep. One time I did it, I had a scary night. Dad, Glen Biles, and others decided to go fishing down on the river, which was about a half mile away. We took bedrolls and other camping equipment. After we set the lines, we went to bed. People were scattered up and down the river bank. About 1:00 or 2:00 in the morning, I woke up somewhere off down the river bottom. It was pitch dark and I had no idea where I was. After stumbling around, I ended up in a ravine. This led me to the river. Eventually, I made my way back to camp.

During the summer of 1925, we were visited by Grandfather Cruzan: David Logan Cruzan, Maud's father and the man from whom I inherited the name "David." He stayed two or three weeks. He took me fishing and I remember him as a very agreeable man. That was the first time I recall seeing him and I never saw him again. Grandmother Cruzan died a few years before I was born so I did not get to know her.

We had two teams of horses at that time (an annual ritual was picking cockle burrs out of the horses' manes and tails in the spring). We also had a modified Model T Ford touring car. Someone had added a station-wagon-type frame (this was pre-station-wagon days). This home-made contraption was great for our big family; all the kids could be stuck in the back.

Getting Dad and the Team Home

That year we raised corn and cotton. The crops were good and prices were good. We would pull cotton all day, and then Dad and I would take the wagon full of cotton to the gin in the evening. We never knew how long we would have to wait, and often we had a lot of time to kill. Sometimes one of Papa's buddies would come along with a bottle. Occasionally there was a crap game in a nearby old garage building where men waited for their cars to be fixed. A few times, late at night, it ended up my responsibility to get the empty wagon and Dad home. Fortunately, if you pointed the horses in the right direction, they generally found their way home.

Near the end of 1925, Dad and some neighbors were playing Pitch. They had probably been drinking some. I don't know what happened, but Dad got angry. He picked up the cards and threw them in the wood heater. End of game!

Another night, Dad had been drinking and decided to leave the house in the Model T. I knew he shouldn't be driving and I followed him outside. He cranked the car, and went around the car to get in. I was on the other side of the car—hidden in the dark. As he climbed into the seat, I crept around to the front. The choke was a little wire on the front of the car. I choked it several times and the car died. Dad climbed out of the car, cranked it again, then headed back to get in. I sneaked around to the front again and choked it to death. This happened several times. Back and forth Dad stumbled. Finally, muttering to himself, he gave up and went back into the house and went to bed.

About this time, I got my first pair of long pants. Up till then, my trousers had been knickers. I felt very grown up!

10

A YEAR TO REMEMBER 1926

In 1926, John L. Baird demonstrated a wireless transmission called "television." Gertrude Ederle became the first woman to swim the English channel. One in every six Americans owned their own car. A favorite song was "When the Red, Red Robin Comes Bob, Bob, Bobbin' Along." Oklahoman Will Rogers traveled Europe as President Coolidge's "ambassador of good will."

For some reason I never knew, in January of 1926, Dad decided to move to Tuttle, Oklahoma, about a hundred miles away. Again, we loaded up the two wagons. Papa took the rest of the family in the car to Aunt Mag's (my mother's sister, Maggie [Cruzan], who had married Noah Sullins). Then Papa left the car there and came back to Mountain View to get the wagons. (How did Papa get back to Mountain View? Beats me.) Again, I drove one and Dad drove the other. It was a two or three day trip to Tuttle.

We lived with Uncle Noah and Aunt Maggie a few weeks while we looked for a farm to rent. While there, we enjoyed getting acquainted with our cousins, Gene and Edna.

Dad finally rented a run-down 160-acre farm seven miles southeast of Tuttle. It had an old dilapidated two-room house with a side-room across the back. It also had a small barn, a drilled well, and the usual path outback. Our family at this time consisted of Papa, Oren, three girls (Hazel, Hester, and Janada), two small boys (Hansel and Troy), and me. Our Indian step-brothers, Sam and W. M. were in the Indian boarding school at Colony, Oklahoma, about fifty miles away.

There was only one rural church near our farm. Dad and Oren never went, but sometimes we kids walked two miles to the building on Sunday evening for the meeting for young people.

MOUNTAIN MAN AND PAPA

For some reason, our neighbor from Mountain View, "Mountain Man" Lander McManus, moved at the same time we did, and rented the place next to ours. We enjoyed playing with the McManus kids. One of the favorite things we did on Sunday was get on the creek bank and "play church." We would sing, preach, and testify. I was the only male, so I got to do most of the preaching.

McManus and Dad generally got along, but once, for some reason, Lander got very mad at Dad. McManus marched up to our fence. Papa was on one side of the fence and he was on the other. We kids were up on the porch. Lander was "cussin'" and fighting mad. Papa told him, "You'd better not cross that fence." Lander hollered, took off his hat and hit the ground with it. Finally, he said, "I'm going to go get my gun!"

Dad came inside to get his gun. Most of us kids thought that was a bad idea, but Hazel said, "If we don't let him have it, he might get shot." So Hazel helped him find the gun and the shells. I guess Lander cooled off though, because he didn't show up that day with a gun.

That spring, my sisters and I attended Union Consolidated School which was a little over two miles from our home. The school had classes for grades one through ten. I was in the sixth grade by this time. One classmate was Bernice Buck, who later married Lee Cruzan. I remember the three Buck girls coming to school *in a buggy*. Wow!

A BANNER YEAR (??)

1926 was "a banner year" for our family—a year when almost everything went wrong. Our old house was infested with rats, rats, rats. Rats got in your bed. One night, a rat (no respecter of persons) bit my nose.

One day a neighbor brought us a nice fat possum, ready to cook. Oren put it on to cook late in the evening with a big mess of sweet potatoes. It didn't get done in time for supper, so she left it in the oven. The next morning the oven door was open and the possum and "taters" had disappeared. Only scraps and bones remained.

We were doubly poor that year. Dad had borrowed money to make the move and it was soon gone (money has a way of doing that). We had enough to eat, but no money to buy horse feed. So we plowed in the morning, and turned the horses out to pasture in the afternoon.

About June, Oren took typhoid fever. In those days, little could be done for the disease. Oren's fever was so high that most of her hair came out. An old doctor from Tuttle got in his buggy every day and made the seven-mile trip to the farm to check on her. He also brought fifty pounds of ice each day for her fever. I doubt if he was ever paid for it. Oren was drastically ill four or five weeks. At times, it was doubtful if she could live. I remember everyone gathered around her bed, wondering if she would make it through the night. But finally the fever broke and she began to recover.

As she started to improve, W. M. came down with the fever. But we had all been vaccinated after Oren got sick, so he had a fairly light case. It was later discovered that the old well on the place was contaminated—by the rats.

About this time, Troy (who was about two years old) had to have an emergency circumcision. We had little gas, but Dad took him about forty-fifty miles in the Model T to Chickasha to the hospital.

We got the cotton planted and had a nice stand. On July 12, we had a great hail, completely destroying our crop. It was too late to replant. So we raised no cotton. We had lost our main source of income.

About September, Oren's sister Odrea and her husband Dood moved to a place about a half mile across the field from us. Oren left us and moved in with Odrea and Dood. It was nothing new for Oren to leave home. (I mentioned earlier the impossible task she took on when she married Dad.) She left three or four times a year. I'm embarrassed to tell you that, whenever this happened, we older kids were tickled. I got to sleep with Papa and the girls got to do the cooking. But this time was different. It had been a rough year and I guess Oren had all she could take. Anyway she stayed away longer. At first, she left her babies Hank and Troy with us, but later she got them. (As usual, Sam and W. M. were in the Indian boarding school.)

The hail that destroyed our crop did not hit a neighbor half a mile away. Once more my sisters and I did not go to the school in the fall. Instead, Papa and we four kids agreed to pick the neighbor's cotton.

We started pulling bolls for our neighbor in October. We had a new experience regarding methods. Our neighbor built two cotton sleds eight feet long, two feet wide, and two feet high. Basically, the sleds were boxes on runners. One horse was hooked on to each sled, and the horses pulled the sleds down the space between the rows.

We walked alongside the sleds and dropped the cotton into them. When the sleds were full, we pulled them to the wagon and turned them over and dumped the cotton onto the ground. The neighbor spent his time picking up the cotton, putting it on the wagon, and tromping it down. There were no scales. We took gin weights. Dad and we four kids pulled a bale a day. We were paid $5.00 a bale.

In late fall, we had some kafir corn to harvest. We had it cut with a binder, put in bundles, and then shocked—about ten bundles to a shock. There was no market for kafir bundles, so we placed a mechanical cutter on the side of the wagon. Stuck in a bundle and chopped the heads off. The grain fell in the wagon and the bundles were left in the field. The heads were hauled to the house and unloaded in a pile.

We then got a young fellow with a homemade thrasher, powered by jacking-up a Model T Ford and running a belt from a wheel of the car to his thrashing machine which had nails inside. It worked—after a fashion. I hauled the grain in a wagon to town and sold it. The bundles we had left in the field were to sold to Uncle Toge Cruzan for $5.00 per thousand bundles.

By the time all the cotton was picked and the feed harvested, it was up in December. We kids had not been to school that fall. Oren was still gone. Papa had had it. "Let's go back to Stratford," he said.

Dad loaded the Model T with the girls and returned to the Stratford area. He rented a sand-hill 40-acre farm near Stratford, one mile north of the McGee School (where the McGee cemetery is now). The 40 acres were no good, but they had a solid little two-room house. Dad came back to Tuttle (still don't remember how), and he and I loaded the two wagons and finished the move to Stratford.

Thus ended 1926, a year that will long live in my memory.

11

A SAD INCIDENT—AND A TRIP TO TEXAS 1927

In 1927, Charles Lindbergh flew solo from New York to Paris, non-stop. The first "talkie" movie was produced: "The Jazz Singer," starring Al Jolson. The first Oscars were awarded. In Oklahoma, Henry J. Johnston became the seventh governor of the state.

When school resumed in January, most of us kids started to McGee School, a two-teacher school. (Hazel and Hester were staying with Grandmother Ada in Stratford.) I was in the eighth grade.

A HEARTBREAKING INCIDENT

Sometime after we got back to the Stratford area, Oren was ready to come home. She had left her sister and brother-in-law, and had gone to live with her mother at Stratford. So Dad went and brought her home.

About March or April, Oren had a baby at home with only Dad present. The baby was stillborn. By the time we got home from school, Dad and a neighbor, Jim Flowers, had buried the baby at the east edge of the farm. Little was said about the birth.

At that time, it was necessary to pass a county exam to be promoted from the eighth grade. When May came, on the day of the exam, the four of us in the eighth grade first walked to McGee, then walked another four miles or so to where the county exams were being given. After we took the tests, we walked back to McGee and then home. My hit-and-miss schooling caught up with me. I failed the exams.

We only planted a few acres of cotton that year, and the boll weevils completely destroyed the crop. We never put a sack in the field.

The place had a flock of Guineas, left by a former renter. The birds had turned wild. They roosted in an old barn and spent their days feeding in a nearby wood. Once in a while, when we needed food, Dad would take the shotgun and kill one of them.

In September, Dad bought a used Dodge car, modified so it was similar to a pickup. We loaded our belongings and headed for the cotton fields of western Oklahoma. We picked cotton all fall for Richard Mandrell, who lived about five miles north of Mountain View. We stayed in a small two-room tar-paper shack near the cotton field. I had my 14th birthday there. While we were at the Mandrells, a bachelor named Jeff—a veteran of WWI—was also there.

Again no school for us that fall, but that didn't worry us kids. We were more used to working than schooling.

A TRIP TO TEXAS!

About December 1, we had finished picking Mandrell's cotton. His father-in-law, Mr. Freeman, lived near Gem, Texas, in the Panhandle of Texas—and he needed his cotton pulled. So we loaded up the Dodge "SUV" and took off. This was my first out-of-state trip. Jeff came with us. He was sweet on Hazel. He had his own car, a Model T Roadster.

We stayed in part of the Freemans' two-story house. They had a small cattle ranch, three miles east of Gem (a "town" consisting mainly of a country store). This was wide-open prairie cattle country—and we got to ride *horses*! As a 14-year-old, I thoroughly enjoyed it. One day, we visited a large cattle ranch. We watched them feed the cattle and had lunch with real live working cowboys.

The Freemans had two girls, 10 and 13, and a boy aged 16 named Johnny. I enjoyed being with Johnny. He considered himself a cowboy and I thought he was very grown-up. But he was having growing pains. One day his dad told him to hush up or he would slap him. Johnny stood in front of his father, threw out his chest, and said, "Hit me. You can't hurt me." Mr. Freeman slapped him clear across the room. I don't know whether it hurt or not, but it did quiet Johnny.

We spent Christmas with the Freemans and continued with them on into January while we finished their cotton.

While at the Freemans, Jeff and I decided that we would do some trapping. We ordered a dozen new steel traps: $1.98 and postage. After setting and running traps for a few days, we caught a skunk. After skinning the skunk and drying the pelt, we sold it for $2.00. That paid for our investment. I could imagine myself the Fur King of Texas. But shortly afterwards, we headed back to Oklahoma. Jeff gave me his half interest in the traps.

12

I LIKED THE SEVENTH GRADE—BOTH YEARS 1928

In 1928, Amelia Earhart became the first woman to fly over the Atlantic. Herbert Hoover ran for President with the slogan, "A chicken for every pot, a car in every garage." Walt Disney's first cartoon introduced Mickey Mouse. In Oklahoma, the Oklahoma City oil field was opened.

We finished the cotton in Gem, Texas, about February 1. We loaded up and came back to Mountain View. We rented a two-room house in town. Dad had rented some cotton land from Mr. Haskin about two miles from town, but it had no house on it.

We kids started to school in Mountain View. Clifford Biles was in the seventh grade. He begged me to go in his class. I wasn't too fond of the eighth grade (remember, I had failed the exams) and I didn't know anybody else, so I went back to the seventh grade to be with my friend. I managed to pass the seventh grade for the second time.

Since we were living in town, we weren't that far from several church buildings, but we seldom attended services. When we did, it was usually a Pentecostal church.

During the summer, after school was out, I worked awhile for a neighbor plowing cotton. He gave me $1.25 a day and dinner. I thought I was rich.

That fall, we kids went to school in Mountain View most of the time (I started the eighth grade again). And our family also made a pretty good crop of cotton.

December 4, 1928, Wanda Jean was born in our house in Mountain View. She was my first half-sister.

Things were going pretty well, but being Ropers, we had to move. The last few days of 1928, we moved from Mountain View to the Lake Valley community, three miles north of Gotebo, Oklahoma.

13

OUT OF THE EIGHTH GRADE—FINALLY 1929

In 1929, Herbert Hoover was inaugurated as the 31st President of the U. S. Gangsterism reached its peak in Chicago. In Oklahoma, Henry J. Johnston was impeached for general incompetence. The lieutenant governor William J. Holloway became the 8th governor of Oklahoma. Most important was the crash of the stock market——and the beginning of the Depression.

GROCERIES

In 1929, a week's grocery bill for my family looked something like this:

- One box Mother's Oats (30¢)
- Six bars of P & G (Proctor & Gamble) laundry soap (25¢)
- One pound of Peaberry Coffee (25¢)
- A 48-pound sack of flour (around a dollar)
- Six small cans of evaporated milk (25¢) (we only had a milk cow about half of the time)
- One pound box of oleo if we didn't have a cow (it looked and tasted like lard until coloring was added; then it was marbly yellow stuff that tasted like lard)
- Three pounds of pinto beans (25¢)
- Matches (package of six large boxes–25¢)

- And three sacks of RJR (R. J. Reynolds) tobacco (25¢) (other options were Velvet and Prince Albert in cans and Bull Durham in 5¢ bags)

We also used lots of cornmeal, but we generally were able to find corn to have ground. When we had a cow, churning was a daily task. My dad churned cream in a half gallon jar every morning.

Biscuits, gravy, and oatmeal was a standard breakfast. The only dry cereal I remember was Post Toasties, which we never had because it was too expensive. Lunch was cornbread and beans—maybe with some fat hog jowl and some home-canned vegetables. Supper was cornbread and milk—if we had milk.

The first of 1929, we "rented" 160 acres from Mr. Albright. The place was in the Lake Valley community, about three miles north of Gotebo, Oklahoma. The land ran along the highway. It was a mile long and a quarter mile wide. We had a small pasture and were allowed a few acres for a feed crop, but mainly we grew cotton. Our agreement was different: One half of the cotton land was on one-fourth shares (we got three-fourths and Mr. Albright one-fourth). The other half of the land was the usual share-crop agreement (half and half). Mr. Albright furnished three horses and we furnished three horses, so we could put together three teams. Albright also furnished the seed and we furnished all the labor.

Three of us kids—Hester, Janada, and me—entered Lake Valley school in January. Hazel had quit school to take a beauty course. She learned how to "marcel" hair. "Marcel" = making waves in the hair with a special "marcel" iron. She heated her iron in a coal oil lamp chimney. Charge for one "marcelling": 50¢. She didn't do much business.

Lake Valley was a rural consolidated school—all twelve grades! Although my family continued to move about once a year, the rest of my grade school and high school work was done in this school.

Hester, Janada, and I rode a school bus with a home-made body and no heat. I was in the eighth grade. In 1929, the superintendent of the school was Byron Dacus. I didn't know it then, but he would later be my brother-in-law.

Around April that year, I took small pox. We were quarantined about three or four weeks. Someone else in the family also came down with a light case. All of us got shots.

In May, I graduated from the eighth grade—finally. This time I didn't have to take the state exams. I think maybe only students in the small country schools had to take those exams.

In May, Sam and W. M. came home from the Indian school. We planted about a hundred acres of cotton, a lot in those days.

In September 1929, I was almost 16—and I started to the ninth grade (the start of high school in those days).

About October, Oren's sister Amy and her husband Bill came and spent the fall with us and picked cotton. We made a good crop—twenty-five to thirty bales.

That was the year of "the bust"—the start of the Depression. We didn't have radio or television, but we knew there was trouble. We heard about people jumping out of windows in New York City. At the beginning of 1929, a bale of cotton sold for $125.00. By the time we sold our cotton, a bale brought less than half that much.

14

THE DEPRESSION GETS WORSE 1930

One of the few bright spots of 1930 was Charles Lindbergh setting a cross-country flying record of just 14 and 3/4 hours in the air. Sliced bread was introduced by the Wonder Bread Company of Battle Creek, Michigan, while Clarence Birdseye introduced quick-frozen foods for the family. The Depression worsened. In Oklahoma, improvements were made in child labor restrictions.

We stayed at the Albright place the next year, under the same arrangement. Mr. Albright was old (to me), 60–70 years at least. He had a law: "Thou shalt not take my horses out of the barn before 7:00 a.m." One morning, Clifford Biles and I went over really early and Albright came storming out. "You are not to take my horses out of the barn before 7:00 a.m.!" I'm afraid I talked back to him. I was 16 and turning into a bratty teenager.

It was a very cold winter. In February, it came a terrible big snow: close to two feet. All east and west roads were closed. We couldn't get to town. School was closed for about two weeks. The nearest store ran out of coal, so Dad had to buy a few sacks of coke so we wouldn't freeze to death. (Coke is made from coal. It burns cleaner, but is more expensive.) We had no cellar so we kept our canned fruit and vegetables in the back room. The jars froze and burst. But we didn't starve.

Dad's uncle Les Thrasher, his wife and their three teenagers had been staying with us when the storm hit and they got marooned. They stayed three-four weeks. Our three-room house was overflowing. Of course, we seven teenagers didn't care. There was no school and we were having fun. As soon as the roads cleared, they left.

The Depression worsened. This "prophecy" made the rounds:

> The world will grow rich and dirty
> And end in 1930.

I remember this ditty:

> 10¢ cotton and 40¢ meat,
> How in the world can a poor man eat?

Actually, the Depression didn't worry us kids that much. I remember the Roper kids and neighbor kids going down on the creek, building a fire, singing and playing around.

THE ODD COUPLE

I mentioned earlier that, in our agreement with Mr. Albright, we had to supply our share of horses so we could put several teams in the field. A good horse or mule might cost up to $100.00, equal in value to two bales of cotton. Renters and tenant farmers could not always own the best, so they often had to make do.

The early part of the Depression, we were short on horse power (I don't remember why). Dad found a neighbor who had an extra horse: a big old bay horse, fourteen hands high, weighing about 1300 lbs. He wouldn't have won a race or beauty contest but he was willing to work. And he was gentle, almost to the point of being lazy. Dad traded a sow and three pigs for Benny—named for the man from whom we bought him.

One more animal and Dad would have a team. He began his search, but being low on funds made the hunt slower. After looking several days, Dad had about decided he was going to have to make a crop with the double-shovel and Georgia Stock. But a horse trader heard about his need for a second horse and came to visit. "I have a good mule I'll sell you," he said. Dad didn't really want a mule to go with his horse but he told the trader he'd take a look.

The next morning Dad went to the man's house. Sure enough, the man had a mule—well, at least half a mule. That animal was the sorriest-looking, scrawniest critter a man ever laid eyes on. He maybe weighed 600 pounds, his tail was matted with cockleburs, and his mane didn't look like it had been roached in years. "Roached" = cutting off the mane of a mule and the top six inches of the hair on its tail; you didn't do this to a horse, but you did to a mule. This unroached mule had a look in his eye that said, "Don't mess with me." The man called him "Babe."

Dad was desperate. It was time to start farming. After much dickering, he traded a calf and fifteen dollars for the poor excuse for a mule.

The next morning, Dad rustled up a collar that would fit Babe and harnessed up the team. As he looked at them, he couldn't resist grinning a little at the mismatched team (Dad seldom laughed out loud). He was hoping the neighbors didn't see them.

It was a hard day. Benny walked slow while Babe was frisky and jumped ahead and then back. It was see-saw all day long with Dad caught in the middle. But finally sundown came. The team was fed and turned out to pasture for the night.

The next morning, Benny was in the lot waiting for his breakfast, but Babe was nowhere to be seen. After breakfast, Dad went looking for the other half of his team. He found Babe a half-mile away, tromping down the neighbor's garden. Back to another day of see-saw plowing. They got through the day.

The next morning, no mule. Dad found him in another pasture, two jumps away. Back to the plow for the third day. A bit better but a long way from an organized effort.

The next morning, no mule. Dad found him again. Dad was a patient man but his patience was wearing thin. All day as he plowed, he pondered the problem of how to keep his meandering mule at home. That evening he took a trace chain about seven feet long, and chained the team together when he turned them out to pasture. Babe didn't like it but he had little chance of dragging big Benny where he didn't want to go.

Next morning, Dad went to feed the animals. Surprise! No mule and no horse! He was shocked. How could that little ol' mule keep that big horse from coming to breakfast?

In the back side of the pasture, he found his team: Babe on one side of the fence and Benny on the other. From the look of things, they had spent the night like that. Dad kept chaining them together at night, but Babe was a slow learner. About every other morning he would find them somewhere separated by a barbed wire fence.

When the crop was laid by, the chain was hung back up in the barn and Babe had free rein again. Sometimes he would visit the neighbors for two or three days at a time. When it suited his fancy, he would jump back into our pasture.

But Babe wasn't through with his meanness. Our milk cow was in the pasture with the working animals. One morning our old Jersey didn't show up. Dad found her with a newborn calf. The calf was barely living; it had been stomped and kicked. For the next two months, the calf had to be lifted up to its mother to nurse. There was no question in anybody's mind that Babe was the culprit.

Had Babe had been abused when he was a mulette? Who knows? Anyway, the calf was finally able to walk and a few months later was turned into meat for a large, hungry family of the depression years. When the cotton was harvested and a little money available, Dad traded the odd couple for a better team. Few tears were shed as Babe was led out of the gate and out of our lives forever.

My third half-brother was born December 21, 1930: Charles Albert Roper, better known as "Buddy." Buddy was the last of Dad's children.

15

A HAIRCUT, A PISTOL, AND A DAY IN COURT 1931

In 1931, the Star Spangled Banner became the national anthem of the U.S. Wiley Post and Harold Gatty circled the world in eight days and fifteen hours. "Alfalfa Bill" Murray became the ninth governor of Oklahoma. He campaigned on the slogan "Just Plain Folks."

In January 1931, we moved a mile south and a mile east of the Lake Valley school. We moved to a 160-acre cotton farm close by the Kelso family. We had a two-room house with two side rooms. We raised a big garden and had a few chickens and hogs. We had more pasture than before. We had two or three old cows and a guy loaned us four or five more. We milked six or seven cows. This was the first time we had cream to sell. We also made our own cheese.

THE HAIRCUT INCIDENT

A man in the community was a pretty fair country barber. He didn't charge anything. He just did it to help people out. Up till then, Dad had always cut my hair but he and I started letting this neighbor cut our hair.

There was another man in the area who was really obnoxious. I'll call him Mr. Smith. He took advantage of everybody and never helped anyone.

One day the barber was cutting Dad's hair when he looked out the window and saw Mr. Smith and two sons walking up. He gave Dad a quarter and told him what to do.

When the barber finished, Papa said, "How much do I owe you?"

"Two bits ought to do it," the man said.

Dad pulled out the quarter and gave it to him.

Mr. Smith jumped up like he had been shot, grabbed his two boys, and said, "Let's get out of here!"

He never came again to get a "free" haircut.

THE DAY I TOOK A PISTOL TO SCHOOL

We kids continued to go to school at Lake Valley. As a timid teenager, I had an inferiority complex. I had few close friends and was especially afraid of girls. One day an opportunity came along that I thought might help my low self-esteem.

Uncle Bill came visiting for a few days. To understand what I did and why I did it, you would need to meet Uncle Bill. He was the husband of Oren's sister, Amy. A "man-about-town" type and a world traveler—at least to hear him tell it. He loved to tell about all the places he had been and things he had done.

One story was how he had whipped the town bully and had taken his gun. He proudly exhibited the evidence, showing a beautiful little pearl-handled, single-shot, twenty-two pistol. A unique gun. One that could impress a sixteen-year-old country boy. As Uncle Bill told the tale with much gusto, I was imagining myself with a gun like that.

The next morning, a brilliant idea hit me: Why not take the gun to school and make an impression on my classmates? No sooner said than done. I stuck the gun in my high-laced boots and pulled the leg of my overalls down over it. It was completely out of sight.

A very excited teenager swaggered toward the school bus, determined to impress his classmates with his grown-up-ness. I couldn't wait to show off. The bus had hardly shifted into high gear before I pulled up my pants leg and exposed the pearl-handled pistol. Boy, I made an impression. I mean, I got their attention!

Once we reached school, the news spread quietly but quickly: "Dave has a gun in his boot." It was a long morning, but finally the noon bell rang. I made a bee-line for the old truck shed—the boys' hangout. I had a good following; they had to see that pistol. I was only too willing to oblige.

I'm telling you, I was walking on cloud nine! Little old insignificant me, the center of an admiring group of my peers. Strutting like a peacock, I told the story of the pistol, embellishing it with a few invented details of my own.

But, alas, too soon the bell rang for afternoon classes. My finest hour was over. Everyone rushed for the building. I lingered behind to put the pistol in the boot.

As I reached the door to the school, who should be standing there? You guessed it. The superintendent! Someone had snitched!

He took my arm and said kindly, "I want to see you in my office." I timidly answered, "Yes, sir," wondering if my knees would hold me up long enough to make the trip. I had never been to the office before, but I had heard rumors about "the torture chamber." Needless to say I was repenting and wishing that I had never seen that pistol. That gun was no comfort to me then.

We walked down the hall. I was in front. I could hear his footsteps: Clomp! Clomp! He was a big man and, by the time we reached the end of the hall, where his office was, I reckoned he was at least ten feet tall! And me—I was a little-bitty mouse about to be squashed!! I thought of stories I had read about condemned murderers walking to the gallows. Boy, I could identify with them!

Finally, after an hour or so (it seemed), we came to a closed door with the words "Office" painted on it. I stopped, wondering if I could bolt and make a getaway. Too late. He nudged me on the arm and said, "Go in." To him, that was a invitation; to me, it was a death sentence.

We went in. "Have a seat", he said. He was a man of few words, but the report was that he was a man of action. Action was what I feared as I collapsed into a chair.

He looked at me with piercing brown eyes. After several minutes (seconds? hours?), he said in a quiet, unassuming voice, "I hear you have a pistol." I sat dumbfounded, wondering what I should say. My feverish mind searched for a way out of the dilemma, but I found none. I finally said, "Yes, sir," praying that my life would be spared until I could tell my parents good-bye.

With those hard boring eyes focused on me, he said, "Let me have it." I reached down, pulled up the leg of my overalls and handed him the beautiful pearl-handled pistol. The pistol that had made me a giant for a little while and then had quickly lowered me to the depth of shame and humiliation.

He took it, laid it on his desk, and said calmly (as if this were a routine, every-day matter), "When school is out, you can come and get the gun. Take it home and don't bring it back." Then his eyes mellowed as he said, "You know you must be punished?" A meek subdued voice issued from somewhere deep inside me: "Yes, sir."

He reached into the drawer where the Board of Education was kept. What happened then behind that closed door? Only two people will ever know.

After school, I took the pistol home and put it back where Uncle Bill kept it. To my knowledge, neither Uncle Bill nor my parents ever knew that his gun was the conversation piece of the day at school.

That was the last pistol-packing excursion I ever went on.

The Depression was getting bad. We made another good crop of cotton, but by this time a bale of cotton was worth only $25.00. We pulled a bale and a half most days. Dad could pull half a bale—a thousand pounds—all by himself. One day we pulled two bales. I pulled eight hundred and one pounds that day—my record. We hauled the cotton to the gin in a short-tongued, iron-wheeled wagon, pulled by our Chevy. Dad would leave for the gin about sundown. He would stay until the cotton was ginned, getting home about midnight or 1:00 a.m. Then he would get up before sunrise for another day of cotton pulling.

Usually the cottonseed from a bale paid for the cost of ginning. Late in the season, about November, Dad would bring home the cottonseed from two or three bales for feeding the cows through the winter. We also fed the cows bundles of kafir corn or cane through the winter (very little hay was baled in those days).

One time we ran out of groceries and Dad went to the Red Cross and got some groceries.

At some point, the government started programs to try to help folks. I remember one where they paid you to plow up every third row of cotton. They also had another program where they paid you to kill your cows and hogs. I think they paid $5.00 a head for cows. You could do whatever you wanted with the dead cows: You could use the meat, give it away, or whatever. We didn't have any beef cattle but our neighbors did and they shared their meat with us. None of us had refrigeration but the government taught women how to use pressure cookers and can the meat.

THE DANGER OF STICKING YOUR NOSE IN

The summer of 1931, I learned the danger of sticking your nose into other people's business. Several of us were in town (Gotebo) when Melvin Kelso and Clifford Biles starting fussing about something. Melvin started calling Clifford a coward. I listened to this awhile, and then said, "Clifford, I wouldn't take that if I was you." Melvin looked me in the eye and said, "Well, what are *you* gonna do about it?" First thing I knew, Melvin and I were squared off—and I wasn't even mad at Melvin. I ended up on the ground, Melvin on top of me, his nose bleeding. I couldn't move, and I had his neck in an arm lock where he couldn't move. So we lay there, his nose pumping blood all over my clean white shirt.

May 31, 1931, Hester married Glen Kelso. In August, Hazel married Miller Cox (three of the Cox boys got married at one time). Our family had gained one (Buddy) and had lost two (Hazel and Hester).

September 1931, I started my junior year at Lake Valley. A teacher came to the school and started a music program. I sang baritone in the boy's quartet. Loys Lee was also in the quartet; he sang tenor. This was my first real association with Loys. He was dating Nova Philley, but I didn't get well acquainted with her until later.

We had two team sports at Lake Valley: basketball and baseball. I was a substitute on the basketball team. I was a fielder on the baseball team.

While in high school, I sometimes went with my friends to a Baptist Church—but not much.

A DIRTY HABIT ACQUIRED

When I was a boy I smoked corn silks and grapevines. Sometime, during my junior and senior years at Lake Valley, I started smoking cigarettes. At first, I snagged snipes (a "snipe" was a partially smoked cigarette someone had thrown down). Eventually I started rolling my own. Dad smoked RJR, but I preferred Country Gentleman—10¢ a bag. By the time I graduated from high school, I was pretty well hooked. It was a habit that I wouldn't shake until thirty or so years later when a lip cancer finally scared me enough to give me the strength to quit.

MY DAY IN COURT

In early December, winter was coming close and it was time to get out the traps and go after fur-bearing critters. For a number of years, I had earned spending money trapping possums and skunks. I went to the barn and took down the traps, the five that were left. I knocked some of the rust off with a wire brush and put oil on them so that, when they were tripped, they would catch whatever tripped them.

After lunch, I headed for a new trapping territory, a neighbor's creek about a mile from our house. The creek was a quarter mile from the home of our neighbor, George, and his family. I walked along the creek bed, looking for likely places to place the traps. I noticed an overhanging bank that seemed a good spot.

I climbed up underneath the bank. There was a darkened hole that looked like it might be a den.

As I stared into the darkness, I saw something unusual: a small whitish object, definitely not something that should be in a hole like that. My first thought was that it was something put there by a pack rat. I timidly reached in and pulled out the object. I held in my hand a new, clean fountain-pen box. I was baffled. When did pack rats start writing?

I slowly, nervously opened the box. Inside were five important-looking pieces of paper, documents of some kind. I had never seen anything like them. I read them, but still didn't know what they were. That ended my trapping for the day. I took my traps and my new-found treasure and headed for the house. My parents looked at the papers but had no idea what they were. (As a matter of fact, they didn't even get excited about my wondrous discovery.)

The next day was Sunday. My brother-in-law, Miller Cox, came by. He had a look but didn't know what the papers were either. He said he was going to town the next day and would take them to the bank in Gotebo. Turned out they were cashiers checks: five $20.00 checks. That doesn't sound like much now, but that much money would have bought ten to fifteen head of cattle or four bales of cotton. Miller turned the checks over to the bank and they said they would do some investigating.

A few days later, I was startled when two men came to the door and asked to talk to me. They were city men, one with a star on his chest. They explained that they were working on a robbery case. An Express Office had been robbed in Kansas a few weeks before and what I had found were Express Cheques that were part of what was taken.

They asked me a lot of questions. I took them down to the creek and showed them where I had found the checks. They searched the area about an hour but found nothing more. They took me home and told me I would need to testify at a trial. They said they had my neighbor George and two other men in jail. That surprised me. This neighbor seemed like all our other neighbors: a nice guy with a nice family.

Testify? I was excited—and scared—about the whole affair. One thing I worried about was facing my neighbor and saying things that might send him to prison.

The law men came a few days later and took me to the court house in Cordell where the trial was in session. Cordell was about fifteen miles from our home. As a teenage country boy, I was in a sweat. I had never been in a courthouse or seen a trial.

I listened for a while and then my name was called to take the witness stand. I was one scared 17-year-old. The bailiff came with the Bible and said, "Place your hand on the Bible." I did.

"Do you promise to tell the truth, the whole truth, and nothing but the truth, so help you, God?"

I weakly mumbled, "I do."

"Please be seated." I was only too glad to do that.

After I told about finding the checks, the defense lawyer began his cross examination by expressing his belief that my brother-in-law and I had robbed the Express Office: "You stole the checks and now you are trying to get my client in trouble!" That hurt my feelings. He continued in the same vein for thirty minutes or so.

As he talked, I looked toward the crowd and there, at the front, sat my neighbor, George. I couldn't look him in the eye. I was thinking about his wife and two little girls without a daddy. I almost wished I could take the blame so he could go home.

After what seemed an eternity, they excused me. Afterward, the sheriff told me that I did real' well: "You didn't let him rattle you." The deputies took me home. I was glad to get there!

I later heard that the men were found guilty and spent some time in prison. I worried about what George and those other men would do to me when they got out of prison. But we moved away at the end of the year and I never saw George again. That's one thing about moving a lot. It's hard to hit a moving target.

I started driving in 1931. We owned a Chevy touring car. One night, late in the year, I came in and forgot to drain the radiator. It froze and busted the block.

In October of 1931, I turned 18.

16

I LOSE ONE FRIEND—AND GAIN ANOTHER 1932

In 1932, Amelia Earhart became the first woman to fly the Atlantic solo. The infant son of Charles and Anne Lindbergh was kidnapped. Franklin Delano Roosevelt was elected president of the United States. In Oklahoma, flamboyant Governor "Alfalfa Bill" Murray's political strength was declining.

In January 1932, the family moved again. Most of the time we moved because Dad had itchy feet, but not always. Dad was known for working hard and cleaning a place up. Sometimes, after he got a place in shape, the owners would think of a reason why he could not stay. This was one of those moves. The family moved to Cloud Chief, Oklahoma, ten miles north of Lake Valley. Dad rented a sorry farm and the sorriest house the family ever lived in.

Janada and I, the only ones in high school, didn't want to leave in the middle of the school year, so we were left behind at Lake Valley. Hazel and Miller were living in the Lake Valley community. They lived in the back two rooms of a four-room house, about three-fourths of a mile (across a field) from the school. Janada and I stayed with them during the spring semester.

When school was out, Janada and I went to Cloud Chief for the summer—to a little three-room house on top of a rocky hill.

The Washita River, which ran across the lower pasture, overflowed seven times that year. When the river was flooding, my younger brothers and I would get on logs and float down the river. I don't know how we kept from drowning. The Washita flooded out most of our crops so we raised little that year. Grandpa Hampy came and found a bee tree and cut it down, so we had honey.

It was deep in the Depression. Few jobs of any kind were available. One day a neighbor hired Oren and four of us older kids to chop cotton. We were thrilled to work for a wage of fifty cents each for the day. Fortunately, we weren't bothered about sales tax, income tax, liability insurance, health insurance, house insurance—or telephone, electrical, and plumbing expenses.

THE PRINCE

He didn't look much like a prince. He was long, tall, lean and raw-boned. He never seemed to eat enough to make him presentable. But it was a different story when it came to disposition. I'm talking about Prince, half of a bay team of horses Dad had bought when I was about seven years old. Prince and Tony. I had grown up knowing, loving, riding, and working those horses. Prince was easy-going, gentle, patient, hard-working, always ready to go the extra mile whether it was plowing or taking the family to town on Saturday afternoon or just giving the kids a ride. On Sunday, we children took turns riding Prince and Tony around the farm. We didn't own a saddle, but an old discarded quilt served the purpose.

Around the end of July in 1932, Dad got a job in the wheat harvest. Many summers, after our crops were laid by, Dad would fix a bundle rack on the wagon and go to wheat harvest. This lasted three to four weeks. He was part of a crew that went from farm to farm threshing wheat. He got $2.00 a day for himself and his team of horses. It was a way for a sharecropper to make a few extra dollars at a time of year when farm income was almost nonexistent. I was eighteen and the oldest boy, so Dad left me in charge.

Everything went well the first couple of weeks. The eggs were gathered by the younger kids. They had been cautioned to handle them carefully. After all, they were selling for 5¢ a dozen. It only took three dozen to buy a box of Mother's Oats or a pound of coffee. The older kids did the milking. We had five cows at the time (did you ever get hit in the face with a cockle-burr-infested cow's tail while milking?). We also separated the cream. Cream was sold each week. Butter fat was bringing 8¢ a pound. With homegrown veggies and the sale of eggs and cream, we got by. (Cokes only cost a nickel—but who had a nickel?)

We worked the horses some in laying by feed for the winter. But mostly we kids enjoyed ourselves. Late afternoons we would go down to the Washita River and take a swim. Following the flooding, the summer had been extremely dry and the river was very low and the river bed was boggy. But we could still find swimming holes.

One Friday evening, after a swim, we started back to the house. We found Tony standing near the trail looking downcast. We wondered why the horse looked so glum. We didn't have to wonder long. As we came around the bend, we were surprised to see Prince standing in the river about twenty feet from shore—up to his belly in thick, soggy, sticky mud. As we watched, he struggled but couldn't move.

Panic hit me. I waded out to the imprisoned horse to see if there was anything I could do. I soon decided there wasn't. The more Prince struggled, the deeper he sank. Finally his back was barely out of the water. We had to have help. I sent brother Hank to a neighbor's house a half mile away.

While waiting for help, I sat on the river bank bemoaning the fact that I had failed in my responsibility. I was supposed to be old enough to care for things and look what had happened!

Thirty minutes later, two neighbors arrived. They waded out to the horse and tried to get him out. No luck. He was going further down with every movement. After a couple hours, the men gave up. They said that there was nothing anyone could do, that the best thing would be to put him out of his misery. They left for home.

Their words stunned me. I sat down. I thought I was too big to cry, so I sat there in silence. I kept thinking, "Surely there's *something* that can be done." Nothing came to mind.

It was getting dark so my brothers, sisters, and I walked slowly up the hill, going home to a supper for which we had no appetite.

I spent a long sleepless night.

At the break of dawn, I got out of bed and got Dad's 12-gauge shotgun. I loaded it and headed for the river, hoping that by some miraculous effort, Prince had gotten out. As I rounded the bank of the river and looked where I had left Prince, my heart skipped a beat. Prince was not there! So he had escaped! I ran a few steps further—and saw him. He had escaped the first grave and had struggled about thirty feet into a worse place. There he stood—exhausted, weak, forlorn.

I stepped into the water and walked to where I could face him. I looked into the beautiful eyes of my old friend. I said a silent prayer, then said good-bye to my Prince. I put the gun to his head. I heard a blast—and he was gone.

It was a long walk back to the house. I was met by my tearful and broken-hearted brothers and sisters.

In a few days, the rains came. The river overflowed—and all traces of Prince were gone.

For some reason, after Sam and W. M. came home for the summer, they spent the fall with the family. In the fall, Albert and Zealin Lowe (Zealin was Dad's baby sister) came and stayed several weeks and pulled bolls.

When it was about time for school to start in the fall, Sam and I both bought a new overcoat out of the Spiegel catalog: $5.00 each!

School started the first part of September—my senior year. Cloud Chief high school was just a mile away. Janada and I went to enroll at Cloud Chief even though we really didn't want to go there. We had our friends at Lake Valley plus I had a girl friend at that school. Officials at the Cloud Chief school sat down with me and said, "We offer this, this, and this." They didn't mention one of the courses I needed to graduate. I didn't ask if they offered that course. Instead, I went home and told Dad, "They're not offering what I have to have to graduate." Dad said, "Well, I guess you'll have to go back to Lake Valley and stay with Hazel and Miller." So Janada and I headed back to Lake Valley. I was a senior and she was a sophomore.

When I got to Lake Valley, I found that my girl friend (who was a year ahead of me in school) had started to college at Weatherford.

LILLIAN IRENE DACUS

But I didn't worry about that long because I discovered that Lake Valley had some new teachers. One was a beautiful 18-year-old first-grade teacher named

Lillian Irene Dacus. She was a sister to Byron Dacus, former superintendent at Lake Valley who was now the County Superintendent of schools. Most just-graduated teachers couldn't find a job at that time, but Byron had personally introduced her to the Lake Valley school board. Lillian had forty-five students enrolled in her primary class and was proud to be paid $65.00 a month. She was staying with Mr. and Mrs. VanDevener, along with four other single female teachers.

I guess I should mention that when Lillian was a child, she had started to school a year early. Then she had skipped a grade while, on the other hand, I had taken the seventh and eighth grades twice. Thus, even though she had been to college two-and-a-half years and had her lifetime elementary teaching certificate, she was a year younger than I.

I should also mention that, to get the job, Lillian had signed a contract that said that she would *not* date any of the students and she would *not* get married.

The first day of the school, we had an assembly during which the new teachers were introduced. The superintendent, who had a sense of humor, had told Lillian that each of the teachers had to make a speech. Actually, all the teachers did was say, "It's good to be here" or "It's good to be back." But he introduced Lillian first. Not knowing any different, she actually made a speech. I thought she looked pretty cute.

We seniors were important people at Lake Valley—at least we thought so. The first week of school, our dignified class of twenty-one had a meeting to decide who our class sponsor would be. The girls nominated the sponsor we had the year before, but the boys nominated the new primary teacher. After much discussion, we decided on Miss Dacus, the old maid of 18 years. We had to get the superintendent's approval regarding our choice. The superintendent-with-a-sense-of-humor went along with it. Part of the committee selected to break the good news to the new teacher was a handsome, dashing, muscular (125# of finely-tuned manhood), brave, young man named Lee David Hamilton Roper.

Jack Ward and I went down the hall to her room. We knocked on the door of her classroom and she opened it. My heart skipped a beat. I was sure we had made a wise selection. We explained our mission and asked if she would accept the honor and responsibility. She accepted the challenge.

I spent a lot of time that year daydreaming about Miss Dacus. I was always available when class business needed to be transacted with the sponsor. (Old dependable Dave!) When she was around, I couldn't keep my eyes off her. When she wasn't, I couldn't clear my mind of her image. I grew sicker by the day—love sick, that is. I made up reasons to go down the hall to confer with our class sponsor. I didn't know if she was impressed, but she was kind and friendly. With the no-dating-students rule, I wasn't sure what to do.

About December of 1932, Hazel and Miller decided that they had to leave Oklahoma and go to Arizona to find work. They finally found work in a lumber camp in Arizona. Janada and I batched in their Lake Valley place the last semester. I mentioned that Hazel and Miller lived in the back two rooms of a house. Actually, it was like two separate apartments. Someone was always living in the other apartment, so it wasn't like we were living entirely alone.

Hazel and Miller had left a little canned food. Then Janada and I got jobs working an hour or so after school each day. Old Mr. Bowden and his wife were the school janitors and they hired us to sweep. We got 10¢ each a day—a dollar a week. With the dollar a week, we bought oatmeal and other necessaries. In addition to this, every week or two, our folks would come and bring us some canned food, milk, and whatever was available. Some weekends, we'd go home to Cloud Chief. We would walk or hitchhike. We would generally bring some meat or vegetables back with us to Lake Valley.

We didn't take any lunch to school. Sometimes we'd find some (if you left your lunch bag on the bus, it was considered fair game), but most of the time we did without. We got by, but we didn't gain any weight. We didn't know we were poor. Besides this, I was in love with the primary teacher, so what did little things like food and clothing matter? After all, I had a house to live in and a bed to sleep in.

Miscellaneous high school stuff: The boys' quartet entered the county contest; I don't remember if we placed or not. I also sang a solo for one program (my one and only solo): "It's Only a Shanty in Old Shanty Town." Mainly I sang as part of a boy's trio that evolved out of the quartet: I sang baritone, Loys Lee sang tenor, and Jack Ward sang lead. We sang whenever and wherever we got together. My wife says we were good and I'm sure she wouldn't lie about something like that. One of our favorite songs began, "After dark when everything is still…."

Occasionally, Dad let me use the car. After the basketball season was over, the coach of the girls' basketball team decided that she would take her girls (ten or so of them) to the Wichita Mountains on a camping trip. I got Dad's car to help haul them and another boy named Gordon had a car. Several of my buddies had "a wonderful idea": They would come on the trip. This sounded good to me: five boys and ten girls sleeping under the stars. The guys would bring their bedrolls and ride in my car. We found a small two-wheel trailer and hooked it to the back of Dad's car to carry the extra gear. When the coach found out about our plans, she hit the ceiling. The trailer was promptly unhooked from the back of the car. The only boys on the trip were the two chauffeurs: Gordon and me.

I turned 19 in October. I continued to admire Miss Dacus from afar. And so the year went.

17

ONE OF THE GREAT YEARS 1933

In 1933, prohibition ended with the ratification of the 21st amendment which repealed the 18th amendment. Top radio programs included The Jack Benny show and The Romance of Helen Trent. Popular songs included "Smoke Gets In Your Eyes," "Inka Dinka Doo," and "Brother, Can You Spare a Dime?" Adolph Hitler became Chancellor of Germany. In Oklahoma, the Fourteenth Legislature enacted the first sales tax.

In January 1933, Dad moved to the Crider place two miles east and one-half mile north of Mountain View, Oklahoma. A three-room house, 160 acres. Mostly cotton.

In the spring of the year, during one of my visits home, I dove into a river without knowing how deep it was. I hit a log about two feet under the water. It had a little spring to it and I popped back up. I coulda broken my neck!

I continued on with my senior year at Lake Valley. After fourteen years and almost as many schools, it looked like I was finally going to do something no one in my family had done before: graduate from high school. But I still didn't know what to do about Lillian Irene Dacus. Sparks were definitely flying between us but the "thou shalt not date students" rule stood like an insurmountable barrier.

Miss Dacus directed the senior play that year and she gave me the leading part. One night during rehearsals, I was sitting in a chair behind the curtains when a girl sat down in my lap. We scuffled a little which apparently caused the curtains to move. Suddenly the curtains parted (at Lil's request, I later learned) and everyone was staring at us. My face must have turned a bright shade of red because everyone else found the situation highly humorous. I gave various reasonable explanations such as "She was exhausted and there was nowhere else for her to sit," and "She fainted and I caught her." Lil didn't seem to be impressed with my explanations.

THE GRAVEYARD EPISODE

The infamous graveyard episode took place in the spring of 1933. A few years ago, when I was jotting down notes on my life, I wrote:

> One night I went out into a graveyard, along with other teenagers. A large tombstone fell on my girlfriend's leg and broke it. Since she wasn't a horse, I couldn't shoot her. So I married her.

But maybe more explanation is in order:

It was March 1, a Thursday. None of the five young unmarried female teachers had a car and it was fifteen miles to Cordell, so someone had to take them shopping. They asked my friend Leonard Kelso if he would take them. He was delighted and invited me to go along. We all loaded into his Chevy and headed to town. One of the teachers was Miss Dacus. The young women shopped until the stores closed. It was dark when we headed home.

We drove back to Lake Valley and dropped four of the young women off at the VanDevener's. But, at some point, Lillian had moved in with the Haynes, who lived another two miles or so farther on—so we headed there to take her home.

It was about 11:00 p.m. when we passed the local graveyard. For some reason—maybe because I was bashful and couldn't think of anything to say—I turned to the Miss Dacus and said, "I bet you are afraid to go into that graveyard." Lil quickly let me know that she was *not* afraid. Leonard stopped the car and we all went into the cemetery, pausing here and there to look at the tombstones. I'm sure I was doing my best to make the situation as scary as possible. It was a small cemetery and we stopped about half way to talk.

Lil leaned over to look at a tombstone, putting her hand (and weight) on it. Then she turned. I'm not sure how it happened, but the tombstone—800–1000 pounds of granite—fell over, knocking her down, and pinning her legs to the ground. Since Lil had been in the process of turning, the left leg was laying across the right leg. The left leg took the brunt of the weight, but the pressure broke the skin on both legs. I thought Leonard and I would never get that headstone off of Lil.

At that point, she was in shock, feeling no pain, just giggling in embarrassment and saying "I'm not hurt." But she couldn't stand up or walk. Leonard and I fixed our arms for a "packsaddle" and carried her to the car. When we reached the Haynes' house, we carried her to the front door. We drove off, feeling terrible.

Lil later told me that it was not long before the pain started and she was aware that something was terribly wrong. We know now that she had a compound fracture; the bone was showing through the skin. But she didn't want to call her folks. She would have to call on a party line and everyone in the community would know what had happened. Also, she was embarrassed. She felt like she had let her family down—especially her brother Byron who had gotten her the job.

The next day, someone helped Lil onto the school bus. Leonard and I met the bus and pack-saddled her into her class room. She taught that day; I don't know how.

The following day, Saturday, there was a basketball tournament forty miles away, at Weatherford, Oklahoma, where Lil had gone to college. She decided to ride the bus with the team to Weatherford so she could see a doctor she had gone to before. When she saw the doctor, he told her that her leg wasn't broken, that she "couldn't stand the pain if it were." He assured her all that happened was that some muscles and tendons were damaged. Then he manipulated her leg and foot until they looked fairly normal and bound them up. "It'll be fine," he said. He took her around the corner to a pharmacist to get crutches. Then the pharmacist, who knew Lil, took her back to the college. She spent a miserable day at the tournament, then rode the bus back to Lake Valley.

Lil spent most of Sunday in bed. On Monday, she again rode the bus to school and started to teach her class. Two or three hours after school started, the superintendent came into her room. "What's wrong, Lillian?"

"I hurt my leg. But don't worry. It'll be all right."

Her leg was swollen and looked awful.

The superintendent went back to his office and called Byron: "What's wrong with Lillian's leg?"

Byron: "Nothing that I know of."

"Well, she's walking on crutches."

It wasn't long before Lil's father and her older brother Zeke showed up. They didn't ask Lil what she wanted to do. After taking a look at her bruised and swollen leg, they packed her up and took her back to Dill City. They suggested taking her to a doctor. She said, "But I've seen a doctor and he said it would be all right."

She was in constant agony. She couldn't stand anything on the leg, so they rigged up a wire frame to keep the covers off. She would cry out in her sleep.

The last of the week, her dad and Zeke couldn't take it anymore. They took her to an unlicensed bone specialist in Corn, Oklahoma. He had studied in Germany, but had not been certified in the U.S. The doctor was horrified at what the first doctor had done. A bone was sticking out of the skin on her left leg and infection was setting in. Both bones in her left leg had broken and they were growing together crooked. He re-broke them (!), set them properly, treated the wound, and put her leg in a proper cast.

Over the weekend, Lil's father and Zeke took her back to Lake Valley. Her older sister Myrtle came with them. Lil and Myrtle got a room in the back of a building near the school. They furnished the room with Myrtle's furniture.

Lil started teaching again on Monday. Myrtle went with her to school each day. Myrtle prepared materials and kept the schoolroom clean—did about everything except teach. When they got back to the apartment, Myrtle did the cooking and cleaning. Every week, Lil's folks took her back to Corn to get the dressing changed on her leg.

I felt terrible about what had happened. I was living three-quarters of a mile away and visited Lil whenever I got the chance. What I had done was stupid, but God in His providence made good come from it. I finally had an excuse to see Lil away from school and "the insurmountable barrier" began to crumble. Our relationship started to get serious. Myrtle liked me and pushed matters from her side. You don't need all the details about my courtship, but among other things (crooner that I was) I sang to her. A Bing Crosby hit at the time was a song named "Please." I remember singing this to Lil. I don't remember all the words, but here's part of it:

> Please lend a little ear to my pleas;
> Lend a ray of cheer to my pleas;
> Please tell me you are not intending to tease;
> Tell me that you love me, too.

LIL, RELIGION, AND ME

As I got better acquainted with Lil, I discovered that she was deeply religious. She didn't preach at me but she read her Bible every day and had a deep faith. Of course that was all right with me. I came from a long line of Roper men who were more than happy for their women to carry the burden of religion. It was mildly interesting to me that she was a member of the church of Christ, the same church my mother had been a member of. But I had never attended that church (at least not since my mother died when I was five) and knew nothing about it.

To use an expression we often heard in Australia, I had "me own religion." The early teachings of my Grandma had stayed with me. And my Dad, though not a church goer, had set a good example of honest everyday living. I had a firm belief in God and in heaven and hell. And I believed in right and wrong, although I didn't always do what I knew to be right. When I didn't, my conscience hurt me. But as far as churches went, I figured one was as good as another—and none of them all that important. But if Lil wanted to be religious, I would follow the example of my forefathers and not stand in her way.

Lil walked on crutches until early May. Then she used a cane. The first day she walked to school without crutches, half the school was out front, cheering her on.

We finally made it to graduation time. My only shoes had big holes in the soles. I wore cardboard in them my entire last year of high school. At graduation time, Lil handed me a graduation present. It was in a shoe box. I was excited. A new pair of shoes! Inside was a fancy brocade bathrobe. A brocade bathrobe for a country boy. A fancy bathrobe for a kid who took a bath once a week—sometimes. But it's the thought that counts.

When school was out, Lil went back to Dill City. Janada and I went home to Mountain View. So Lil and I were 25–30 miles apart, a *long* way at the time. Lil's folks had a phone, but we didn't, so we couldn't stay in touch that way.

But things were looking up some for our family in general. The farm Dad had moved to was a pretty good one. Dad had given me a five-acre patch of ground to plant cotton. Dad helped me plow it, but I had to do the hoeing and the rest of the work. From May until July, we planted, chopped, and plowed our cotton crops.

One evening, Janada and I borrowed Dad's car and drove to Dill City to see Lil, but she had taken her brother Zeke into the mountains near Roswell, New Mexico, for his health. Several weeks later, one hot night in July, at 9:00 in the evening, I was already in bed. A car pulled up outside and honked. Haskell and Myrtle had brought Lil to see me. They visited a couple of hours and then drove back to Dill City. It was the first time I had seen Lillian since school was out.

A LUMBER CAMP IN ARIZONA

About mid-July, we laid the crops by. Hester and Glen had been living a quarter mile from us across the field, in a half-dugout. They decided to go to Arizona, to the lumber camp where Hazel and Miller were, to try to find work. At the time, they had one baby, Ronald. Glen's older brother Carl and his wife and their four-year-old girl decided to go with them. Janada and I decided we might as well go too.

Hester and Glen had a two-door Chevy and a two-wheel trailer behind. Clifford Biles wanted to go, too, but it was decided that eight was the limit. Clifford offered to lay on top of the trailer and travel there the four or five days necessary to make the 1200 mile trip, but his offer was declined.

The eight of us piled into the little car and took off. It was July with no air conditioning in the car, but no one worried about it. That's just the way it was. If there were any motels, we didn't know about it—and couldn't have afforded to stay in them anyway. At night, we spread our bedrolls by the side of the road and slept there.

When we reached Flagstaff, Arizona, we started driving into the mountains. The lumber camp was about sixty miles north of Williams, Arizona. The camp was about ten miles from the rim of the Grand Canyon. It consisted of little shacks scattered on the mountainside. Thirty to forty men lived in the shacks.

They cut down the trees and hauled them to a small-gauge railroad that took the logs to Williams.

Miller already had a job there and Glen got one. Carl finally got a job washing dishes. I didn't get a job.

THE DAY I STARTED A FOREST FIRE

One day we needed wood for the cook stove. Carl and I drove the car and trailer into the forest to get wood. As we gathered the wood, we were smoking. We filled the trailer and headed back to the camp. The next morning, forest rangers showed up and started measuring the wood in our wood pile. They asked, "Did you cut this wood?" Then they added, "Whoever cut this wood started a forest fire."

Apparently our cigarettes had started a fire. Fortunately, someone came along soon after the fire started and put it out. When the forest rangers appeared on the scene, they measured the stumps of the trees that had been cut—which they matched to the wood in our wood pile.

The rangers said, "Do one of you want to confess?" Carl was working and I wasn't, so I confessed. The rangers put me in their car. I was scared to death. I had never been arrested before. They drove me fifteen miles to ranger headquarters. They went into the building and left me sitting in the car. For an hour or so. Finally they came back out. One of them said, "Well, the judge is not in right now. And we don't know when he will be back. Tell you what—if you promise never to do this again, we'll let you go." I started licking his shoes and promising.

And I've kept my word. I haven't started a forest fire since.

MY GRAND CANYON ADVENTURE

I continued to lay around the camp with no job. There was another fellow in camp who had arrived shortly after we had—a forty-year-old bachelor from Lake Valley named Bill Fessure—and he hadn't gotten a job either. One day Bill said that he would like to go down to the bottom of the Grand Canyon and explore a little. He said it was about a mile to the bottom of the canyon and that the trail down was eight miles long. It was an intriguing thought.

So we made our plans. Miller agreed to take us the ten miles to the canyon. We gathered what supplies we could find: some biscuits and bacon, a can of

beans, a coffee can, a skillet, a couple of bedrolls, and water. I also found a package of tapioca in Hazel's cupboard and threw that in. Extra clothing was not a
problem since it was early August.

The trail down started near ranger headquarters. We arrived there about 10:00
a.m. The trail down was called the Bright Angel Trail and was well-marked.
Tourists made the trip the year round. Most of them rode mules down and back,
but we were going to walk.

Down we started. At first it was fun. We were going downhill; it was easy. It
took no effort, except that we had to hold back a little. But after an hour or so, I
began to feel tension in my leg muscles and it slowly got worse.

About half-way down, we came across a small building. We rested a bit, ate
some of our lunch, and then started down again.

We met some teenage city dudes coming back. They were a sad-looking lot,
almost at the point of tears. "Turn back!" they said, "Don't go any further! You
can't make it!" We rugged country men laughed at them and continued on.

We made it to the bottom before sundown. We cooked our supper on a
campfire on an open spot on the bank of the Colorado River. Since we were short
on supplies, I stuck the tapioca in a skillet and added water. That's the first and
last time I've eaten fried tapioca. We were exhausted so we spread our bedrolls
and went to sleep.

The next morning, we cooked breakfast and started back up about 8:00 or
9:00. We reached the halfway point about noon. We were tired but kept going.
On the way down and the way up, we met several mule trains: eight to ten folks
on mules with a guide. We reached the top before dark and someone picked us
up.

MY FIRST TIME TO RIDE THE RAILS

Altogether I was at the lumber camp about three weeks. Two or three days after
The Grand Canyon Adventure, Bill and I decided to ride a train back to Oklahoma. Bill had ridden the rails before, but it would be a First for me.

We made preparations for the trip. I had a small pack of clothes (overalls and
a light jacket). Bill made up a bedroll with some worn-out quilts my sister gave
us. Bill had no money. I had two dollars that Hazel had given me (two days wages
for Miller!). This was the first money I had had on the trip. I don't think Bill
knew I had it. I got home with some of it.

On the morning of departure, we walked down to the railroad (a small-gauge line that hauled the logs), said our farewells and waited for the daily logging train to take us to Williams, Arizona. Excited? I couldn't sit still thinking of that great big beautiful world out there waiting to be conquered by an inexperienced, uninformed, and ignorant farm boy from the cotton-fields of Oklahoma.

The train finally arrived, and stopped for a few minutes. When it pulled out, one experienced hobo and one scared teen were sitting on a flat car, surrounded by pine logs, heading for home 1200 miles away.

We arrived in Williams late in the afternoon. Williams was situated on the main line railroad. We walked up the railroad about a mile and located a slight grade where the through train would have to slow down. We decided this was the place to get on.

The sun was still up so we walked back to town to find something to eat. I went into a bakery and asked, humbly and politely (and frightened to death), "Sir, do you have any work I could do for something to eat?"

The owner replied, "Get out of here, you bum!"

As soon as I stopped shaking, we went to a house just off the main street, and Bill tried his luck. The lady gave each of us a big plate of mutton. I had never eaten any mutton, but I was so hungry that it tasted great. We spent the night bedded down by the tracks.

About sun-up the following morning, the train came. Bill had instructed me how to catch the train: catch the ladder on the front end of the boxcar. We caught it safely and climbed up on top of the boxcar. We sat in the sunshine, the train rattling beneath us, headed for home.

About the middle of the afternoon, we pulled into the station at Grants, New Mexico, to take on water. A bull (the nickname for a railroad security officer) walked toward us and told us to get off and not to get back on. We got off but, a short time later, climbed back on. This time we found an empty boxcar to crawl into.

Some time during the night, the train pulled into Clovis, New Mexico. We were awakened by a big burly bull hitting the floor of the boxcar and yelling at the top of his lungs, "Get out of there!" (The rest of what he said is unprintable.)

He lined up the riders he found, about seven or eight of us. He started at the other end of the line, asking our names, where we lived, where we were going and why, etc. He came down the line. I was shaking and shivering. I knew he would hit me with that big stick when he came to me. By my side was a kid, maybe 16, even more scared than I. The bull asked him who he was. He answered with a quivering voice, "My name is _____. I'm going home. And I'm going to stay there when I get there!" For some reason, his voice and answer didn't suit the bull, and he gave him a first-class cussin' out.

I was next. My breath came in short gasps. My knees were knocking. I knew he could hear my heart pounding. I said a short prayer. But instead of bawling me out, he turned and walked back to the other end of the line. He said, "You bums, get out of this yard! You are *not* catching the next train out!" We turned and scattered in all directions.

Bill and I went about a hundred yards from the track and lay down until dawn. About sunup, we heard the whistle of a train. We grabbed our stuff and ran for the tracks. The train barely slowed as we approached. I grabbed for the bottom step of the ladder and caught it and climbed up on the train. I looked back and saw Bill standing by the track. He had missed the ladder. It hit me: I was *alone*.

At Sweetwater, Texas, I got off the train to give Bill a chance to catch up. I slept that night in an empty boxcar. The next day I went to the edge of town to a small lake. I took a bath and washed my socks. I waited all day—no Bill. I never saw Bill again.

That evening, a train came through—headed for Fort Worth. I arrived in Fort Worth in a downpour. I walked across town to a soup line that some hobos told me about.

The next day I caught a train north to Chickasha, Oklahoma. From Chickasha, I hitchhiked forty miles west to Mountain View. I had taken seven days to travel 1200 miles. I was tired, dirty, but wiser (kinda).

GO TO COLLEGE? WHY NOT? NOTHING ELSE TO DO

Few jobs were available for high school graduates, especially in rural areas. I couldn't find any work around Mountain View, so after about a week I hitchhiked to Lake Valley to see what I could find. I had no great plans. I had an extra pair of overalls and an extra shirt with me.

When I reached Lake Valley, I contacted Jack Ward. Jack couldn't find work either. We decided we would go to Goodwell, Oklahoma (350 miles away), to Panhandle A & M (Agricultural and Mechanical) College, to go to college. Byron Dacus, former superintendent at Lake Valley, was now the president of Panhandle A & M, and several other Lake Valley kids had already gone there. We figured maybe Mr. Dacus could help us.

Jack's sister was visiting her parents. That night she took us back to her home in Rocky (about ten miles). The next day we hitchhiked fifty miles or so to Sayre, Oklahoma, to catch a freight train.

JACK AND THE THREE SHELL GAME

It was a hot, sweltering day in August. We reached Sayre about 5:00 o'clock and wandered down to the rail yard. There were several other bums/hobos waiting for the freight train to pull out.

Under the shade of a tree sat a nice looking little old man. He had a board on his lap and on the board were three walnut shell halves. The man was quietly entertaining himself by moving the little shells around. We were fascinated. We had never seen the like before so we walked closer and watched.

He continued to slowly move the shells around. Finally he took a little round piece of rubber from his pocket and placed it under one shell, and continued to move the shells. He noticed us watching him. He looked up and said, "Can you tell me where the little ball (that's what he called it) is?"

Before I had a chance to speak, Jack yelled, "I can."

The nice little man said, "Show me." Jack—being the eager beaver type—quickly reached down, picked up a shell and, sure enough, there was that little ball!

The kind little man said, "Son, you've got a quick eye." Jack beamed with pride. After all, he did have a high school diploma.

The man continued his fascinating game while Jack watched him like a hawk. Again the man asked Jack if he could find the ball. Jack reached over and, sure enough, he picked up the right shell!

The sweet little man decided the fish was hooked and he best drag him in. He asked Jack whether he would like to bet him a dollar that he could tell him where the little ball was. Jack's eyes lit up like a Christmas tree, but they fell just as quickly. "I don't have any money," he said. He spoke the truth for neither of us had a nickel.

The man wasn't perturbed. He just slowly continued to move his little shells. All of a sudden, Jack got a cunning look in his eyes. He said, "I'll bet you my new class ring against the dollar that I can tell you where the ball is."

The man hesitated, looked at the ring (valued at about $10.00), moved the shells a few more times and then said, "All right, but if you don't find the ball, I'm going to keep your ring."

Jack was beaming! An easy dollar (a dollar was a day's wages)! He took off the ring, laid it on the ground beside the man's dollar bill and confidently reached for the shell. He picked it up and—you know "the rest of the story"—no rubber ball. It had vanished.

It's hard to find words to describe the look on Jack's face. Unbelief, shock, bewilderment, agitation. He was speechless, quiet, dumbfounded—however you want to say it. The sweet little ol' man, no sympathy in evidence, reached over and picked up the ring.

Jack, being a smart boy, started thinking hard and all of a sudden he came alive again. His eyes gleamed. His countenance glowed with his bright idea. Quick as a flash, he said to the dear little friend who was wearing his ring, "I'll bet my shoes against the ring that I can find the ball this time!" Life has some hard lessons, but Jack hadn't learned his yet.

But the story didn't end all bad. The dear, sweet, friendly little man refused to take Jack's shoes. As the freight train pulled out, we were on it—less one class ring but wiser in the ways of the world, and especially to the little shell game.

Late in the afternoon, the freight train pulled out for Amarillo, Texas—about two hundred miles away—with all us hobos on board. I was riding the rails again. We curled up in a corner of an empty box car and, in spite of the racket and rocking, went to sleep. During the night, we arrived in Amarillo. Early the next morning, about sunup, we caught another train, this one going to Canadian, Texas. This time we were not so lucky. The train was moving fast and we didn't see an empty boxcar, so, as a last resort, we jumped on an oil tanker. Even though it was August, the nights on the high plains were cold. We had no coats and no place to sit. So we spent the night hanging on the railing. It was a rough, cold ride!

We arrived in Canadian, Texas, about 9:30 a.m. We hadn't had anything to eat since we left home. We were cold, dirty, exhausted, and *hungry*. We jumped off the train. "We've *got* to find something to eat." We had limited experience at begging food but had to learn fast. Desperation gave us courage. We knocked on the door of the first house we came to and told the woman our story. We stuttered and stammered but she got the idea. She invited us in and fixed us a nice breakfast. I don't think I've ever enjoyed a breakfast so much.

After eating, we walked to the highway at the edge of town and started hitchhiking. It was about 10:30 a.m. We made it to Perryton, Texas, about 1:00 p.m. A big frontier celebration was going on. We walked around, watching the festivities. Would you believe it, Jack ran into a friend he hadn't seen in a long time.

After visiting awhile, he asked if we had eaten any lunch. Easy answer. He insisted on feeding us. Two meals in one day! The Lord looks after children and idiots! I'm not sure which category I fell into that day.

After lunch, we went back to the highway. We walked most of the afternoon. A man came along in an old truck. "I'm going about thirty or forty miles," he said. We crawled in. He dumped us out thirty miles from nowhere. Not a house in sight. The few cars that passed weren't interested in giving us the time of day. About sundown, we came to an old country schoolhouse. We tried the door. It wasn't locked. We decided to spend the night there. We lay on the bare floor. No bedroll and no supper, but we slept soundly.

The next morning, we were back on the highway, hitchhiking. We made it to Goodwell about sundown. It had taken us three and a half days to travel some 350 miles. We looked up two friends who were going to college there. They took us in and fed us. We cleaned up some and went to bed.

The next day we borrowed clothes from our friends and went to talk to the president, Lil's brother Byron. He was very helpful. He said one of us could go to work immediately (20¢ an hour, eight hours a day, until school started) while the other went back home for spare clothes and other supplies. I was elected to stay. I stayed with the friends and worked for two weeks until Jack returned. He had gathered up a few clothes, some canned goods, and some fresh vegetables. He brought me an extra pair of overalls, two old shirts, and an old jacket.

Jack and I set up housekeeping with the friends—in two tiny rooms in a basement. Our room rent was $2.50 a month, including utilities. We had an outdoor toilet and took our baths at the athletic dressing room at the college. We took turns cooking. We couldn't afford store-bought bread so made flap-jacks for every meal. When we could get hold of left-over stale bread, we had breaded tomatoes. We would dump a jar of home-canned tomatoes in a pan, add some bread and a little sugar, and heat it up. We would eat the bread and then add more bread to the tomatoes for the next meal.

Goodwell was a small town with two grocery stores. One was owned by Tom Rayburn. He had a panel truck that he drove to Guymon ten miles away most every day to pick up merchandise. This panel truck was the free bus line for the students. Anyone who wanted could ride to Guymon and back with Tom. The truck was generally packed with students. I think I went with him once.

Classes started September 11. After school started, I kept the same college job but had to cut back on the hours. Loys Lee and Nova Philley also started to Panhandle A & M that fall.

When I started to school, I thought I would get in the banking business. As the son of a sharecropper, each spring Dad had to go to the bank to get money to live on and make another crop. It had been drilled into my mind that banks were where the money was. And you had to have money if you were going to buy a farm. I never understood it—still don't—but you could buy a house in town with very little down and pay it out. But if you wanted a farm, you had to pay a fourth or a third down. Money was the key.

So I started as a business major. I took typing, business English, and any other course I thought would lead to a bank full of money. "Me Big Chief Banker." That pipe dream lasted about a semester. Then I switched to something I was more suited for: an agriculture major—animal husbandry. I share these details in case you wonder why I did not end up a wealthy banker or world-famous financier.

A few days after school started, I walked by a notice board and saw "Wanted: Band Members." There had been no band at Lake Valley, but I always figured I could make a great musician. I told you earlier about the harmonica I had when I was small. I hurried to the designated office and asked about the band. The lady in charge said, "We only have one instrument left: a baritone horn." I said, "I'll take it." She handed me the Monster. I had been thinking of something more the size of a Jews Harp. Anyhow I accepted the thing and headed for our little apartment. I had never even picked up a band instrument before. I started blowing. The other fellows came in and fixed their supper, but I kept blowing. This continued until I was worn out—about 11:00 p.m. My roommates called a caucus and decided that the horn or I had to go. The next day I sadly ended my band career.

College life was not particularly exciting, but it was different. Nobody was around to direct your activities with "Time to get up," "Get to class," "Study," "Do your homework," "Get to bed," and all that stuff. I could hang out until late and then sleep in and miss class. I thought I was getting by with it until grades came out: a "D" in college algebra. My first "D"! But I slowly learned what college was all about.

Lil and I were writing letters to each other, but I still dated some. On one of those dates, I greatly embarrassed myself. The girl was a cute little blond named Thalia Pearson. It was the first or second time I had gone out with her. A joke was making the rounds where a guy says to a girl, "Let's get married," and the girl replies, "OK, but who'd have us?" On the date, I ran out of clever things to say—and thought of the joke. I said to Thalia, "Let's get married."

"Oh no!" she said, "We're too young…and we've just started college…and we can't afford it"…and on and on.

I felt like a heel.

October 5, 1933, I turned 20.

In October or early November, Lil came to Goodwell for a weekend. She stayed with Byron and we spent some time together. I promised her I would come home for Thanksgiving.

The day Panhandle A & M turned out for Thanksgiving, one of my roomies named Woody, who lived in New Mexico, said, "Why don't you go home with me for Thanksgiving?" I'd never been to New Mexico. It would be An Adventure. On the spur of the moment, without thinking (I did a lot of that), I said, "Sure!"

We had already heard a freight train at the nearby tracks. I grabbed a coat and we ran for the train. The train hadn't been rolling but a few minutes when it hit me: "I was supposed to go home!" About midnight, we arrived at Woody's home in New Mexico. He lived on a ranch and his folks were nice, but it was a long, miserable weekend for me because of my guilty conscience. On Sunday we caught a freight train back to school.

I spent much of Monday writing a long letter to Lil, begging forgiveness for being forgetful and for my rash decision. I'm told that she exploded when she found out what I had done. I just about blew the whole deal right there.

OUR "SECRET" MARRIAGE

When college turned out for Christmas, I went back to Mountain View. I had a lot to tell them since I was the first in my family to attend college. The family helped me pull a bale of cotton from the five acres Dad had let me use. After the bale was sold and rent taken out, I had $25.00 left. I put the money in my pocket and borrowed Dad's 1928 Chevy coupe.

Clifford Biles went with me to Dill City on December 26. We arrived at the Dacus farm just before dark. Lil, the farmer's beautiful blue-eyed daughter, rushed out in her overalls to open the farm gate. My heart beat faster. Why, oh why, had I gone to New Mexico? I drove through the gate, jumped out of the car, and started apologizing. She graciously forgave me and we enjoyed our reunion. And made some serious plans.

We spent the night at the Dacus' home. The next morning, without saying anything to her folks what we planned to do, Lil left with me and Clifford and we went back to Mountain View. On the 28th, a Thursday, we told my folks that we were going to visit Grandma Ada. Janada, Clifford, Lil, and I started for Stratford. Lil and I had our best clothes with us. It was misty and rainy all day.

We got to Anadarko, Oklahoma, thirty to forty miles down the road. We figured no one would know us there—and that it was far enough from Lake Valley where they would not find out if Lil and I got married. (Remember those restrictions about dating students and getting married.)

We arrived at Anadarko around noon. We found a hamburger joint and spent some of the cotton money there. A burger and fountain drink was a special treat. After lunch, we headed to the courthouse to get a marriage license. I had to lie about my age; I said I was 21 (boys had to be 21 and girls 18 to get a marriage license without parental permission). The license cost $3.00.

We changed into our best clothes in the courthouse restrooms. Then we started driving around, looking for someone to marry us. About 2:00 p.m., we saw a sign in front of a Methodist preacher's house indicating he performed weddings. The ceremony took place in his house. Janada and Clifford were witnesses. Afterward I asked the preacher, "How much do I owe you?" He said, "The state allows me to charge $2.50." That's what I gave him.

We still had 50–60 miles to go to get to Grandma's house. About 8:00 or 9:00 p.m., we were west of Pauls Valley, out in the country. It had been rainy all day and, when I tried to cross a small creek, we got stuck. I saw a light in a house a quarter mile or so down the road. I walked to it and told a farmer my sad story. He brought his mules and pulled the car out of the creek. He wouldn't take any money.

We arrived in Stratford about 10:30. We were tired—but married. We were greeted warmly by Grandma and Grandpa and by Aunt Zealin and Uncle Albert Lowe, who were there for the night. Lil and I spent our wedding night on one of Grandma's feather beds.

We were at Grandma's all day Friday. That evening Grandma just had to have a wedding shower for us. She gathered in everyone she knew.

On Saturday, December 30, we drove back to Mountain View to tell my folks what we had done. We dropped off Clifford. Then Lil, Janada, and I went back to Lake Valley. Lil had moved again—she and Janada had been batching at Hazel and Miller's home—and that was where we were headed. A half mile from our destination, we had a flat tire. It was late and we were tired, so we left the car in the middle of the road and walked the rest of the way.

I had made arrangements to go with Loys and Nova back to Goodwell. They had gotten married a few weeks earlier, on the Thanksgiving break, and Nova's mother was taking them and me back to school. I got up early Sunday morning and walked a mile to Lake Valley where I would be picked up.

So I left my new bride. Left her three days after we got married. Left her to break the news to her family about our marriage. Left her with a borrowed car with a flat tire. (Lil got Miller Cox's brother to go after the car. By the time he got there, someone had stolen one of the tires.)

18

SO MUCH FOR TRYING TO KEEP A SECRET! 1934

Shirley Temple made her first full-length movie—at the age of 6. Another successful movie was "It Happened One Night." Bonnie Parker and Clyde Barrow were gunned down in Texas. "Baby Face" Nelson and "Pretty Boy" Floyd were also killed. Drought hit many parts of the country—including the panhandle of Oklahoma—resulting in the infamous "Dust Bowl." Ernest W. Marland was elected as the tenth governor of Oklahoma.

January, 1934, I was back in Goodwell, secretly married, while my wife was in Lake Valley. The plan was for Lil to finish out the year at Lake Valley and then we'd publicly announce our wedding.

A week or so after school resumed at Lake Valley, an eighth grade girl came to Lil and whispered, "You got married. I saw it in the Anadarko paper." This made Lil uneasy. As time went by, she felt worse and worse about the deception. In February, she resigned. Zeke brought her to Goodwell. So much for our secret wedding.

WE START MARRIED LIFE

By the time Lil got to Goodwell, she had little money and I had none. But she did bring a few jars of home-canned fruits and vegetables, and I had a part-time job with the college. Lil's brother Byron Dacus, president of PAMC, had to go to Oklahoma City once a month for a board meeting of Oklahoma colleges. He generally spent one night with his parents and they would send food back to us: cornmeal, home-canned vegetables, home-canned fruit (plums, peaches, apples, apricots, blackberries), fresh fruit and vegetables in season, and maybe some milk and meat. Lil babysat for a neighbor for a quart of milk a day. When you are young and newlywed, it doesn't take much to get by. We didn't know any better than to be happy.

We rented a one-room apartment, a bedroom really. We rented from "Grandpa" C. W. Reid, a widower 60–70 years old. The room cost us $6.00 a month. It had electricity, a little bedroom gas heater, a two-burner hot-plate, and a little bookcase that we used for a cabinet. We had to go through his house to get water from his kitchen. The toilet was outside. We stayed there until school was out in the spring.

Tuition cost $4.00 a semester plus $1.00 lab fees. In May, I got a Federally-funded student job that paid 30¢ an hour. My college job was with the Agricultural Experiment Station. Our "horsepower" on the station was a No. 10 Caterpillar and a pair of draft horses. Among other things, we were testing different varieties of small grains (wheat, oats, etc.) to see which would present the best yield under Dust Bowl conditions. Water penetration in the soil was a big concern, so we did soil samples every Saturday. I was also the weather man—checking the measuring devices every day. I attended classes in the morning and worked five hours each afternoon and all day on Saturday.

After Lil arrived, I started qualifying for my teaching certificate. Lil was a teacher, so it made sense for me to be a teacher, too.

Byron and several faculty members were members of the church of Christ, and they had started meeting in an old store building downtown. J. Harvey Dykes, one of my science teachers, did some of the preaching. Lil attended there and I went with her most of the time. That was my first exposure to the church of Christ.

By the time school was out in the spring of 1934, Lil was pregnant. She went home to Dill for several weeks to be with her family. While she was gone, I batched with some boys. When she came back, we moved into the basement of a rooming house called "The Brick," owned by "Aunt" Minnie Ginns.

I worked for the college all summer and made some extra money. My income for 1934 was $337.50. Groceries cost us about ten dollars a month (10¢ would buy two pork chops). We didn't have a car.

About the last of August, we and the Lees came up with A Great Plan. We decided to rent an old house, live together in part of it, and rent out the other part to college students. The house we rented was basically a two-room dwelling with three tiny side rooms—one of which was the kitchen.

Neither the Lees nor we had a car—and we didn't have any friends with cars—so we moved using the crib we had bought for our on-the-way baby. We would fill the crib (which had wheels) with our belongings. Then Loys would get on one end and I would get on the other, and we would push it through downtown Goodwell to the rented house. Back and forth we went.

We rented half the house (the larger room in the back and one small side room) to four college boys from Lake Valley: Jack and Tink Ward, Leonard Kelso, and Rex Bowen. Loys, Nova, Lil, and I lived in the other half.

There was a big open doorway between the front room and the back room. The railroad tracks were fifty feet or so behind our house. Near the tracks was a stack of panels used with boxcars hauling grain. We borrowed a couple of panels, nailed them over the door, and put a curtain over that.

Loys and Nova slept in a back porch room with barely room for a bedstead. Lil and I slept in the front main room that was living room, dining room, and study room for the four of us. We shared the kitchen.

Living with Loys and Nova turned out to be more expensive than I anticipated. They did everything they could to make sure expectant Lil ate right. They also wanted to satisfy her every craving. One thing she craved was watermelon. In the middle of the Dust Bowl days, watermelon was *expensive.* But they bought her a watermelon. Their intentions were the best, but we were splitting the food bill down the middle. They could afford it, but we couldn't.

Speaking of bills, we shared the utility bills with the college boys. One of them had the bright idea of adding a little piece of copper wire where the electricity came into the house, causing most of the current to bypass the meter. They kept track of the meter reader's schedule and would remove the extra bit before his monthly visits. I'm not proud that I let them get by with this. But low electric bills did help us survive.

MY FIRSTBORN

My first son came into the world in this small house crowded with eight adults.

November 14, 1934, at 3:00 a.m. in the morning, Dr. Haynes from Guymon, Oklahoma, and Aunt Minnie Ginns (our former landlady) delivered a baby boy—weight nine and a half pounds. He was named for me (David) and for his Grandpa Roper (Lee): David Lee Roper. (By a happy coincidence, his middle name was also the last name of our best friends.)

During the delivery, I almost fainted. I had delivered many calves, pigs, and lambs, but for some reason this affected me differently. Aunt Minnie had to help me outside where I proceeded to try to throw up. Years later, after David was grown, I wrote him this note: "We paid the nurse $10.00 for prenatal care and the doctor $10.00 for the delivery. You were expensive!" I added a P. S.: "The father was the sickest one during the whole ordeal!"

While all this was going on, Loys was back in their tiny room while Nova was in the middle of the proceedings.

As already mentioned, there were only panels and a thin curtain separating our room from the room where the college boys slept—so they got the night-time excitement in wrap-around stereo. At 7:00 the next morning, they showed up on our side of the house, clean and scrubbed, hair slicked down, to welcome my new son.

You would have thought that David was Loys and Nova's child, the way they played with him and took care of him. I don't think Nova had been around babies much, so everything David did fascinated her. Once, while changing his diaper, she got a face-full, but she thought it was funny. David's first smile and first laugh was for Loys and Nova. Of course there were the usual baby problems. David had the three-month colic. He cried every night for three months to a day. Then he stopped, just turned it off.

TRYING TO KICK THE HABIT

The birth of David Lee made me think serious thoughts. I wanted to raise him right. One thing that concerned me: I didn't want him to smoke. Both Loys and I smoked, but we pledged to quit in order to be a good example. I don't know how long Loys lasted, but I made it only a few days without a cigarette. Then I started sneaking a smoke now and then behind the outhouse. One day when I walked behind the outhouse, Loys was there—smoking. So much for good intentions. (Incidentally, David never did smoke. Could our good intentions have helped???)

We stayed with the live-with-the-Lees arrangement for only one semester—until Christmas. Lil and I then moved to a basement room in Mr. Mitchuson's apartment house. We lived there the rest of that school year.

19

THE DUST BOWL—AND THE WPA 1935

The WPA came into existence. The Social Security Act was signed into law. Elvis Presley was born. Amelia Earhart, who had previously conquered the Atlantic Ocean, was the first woman to fly over the Pacific. The top radio program was Fibber McGee and Molly. In Oklahoma, 150,000 heads of families were unemployed; 800,000 were on relief. 61% of Oklahoma farms were operated by tenants (renters or sharecroppers).

I continued attending college at Panhandle A & M in 1935. I sang in the Boys Glee Club and in the Acappella Choir.

AN EMBARRASSING INCIDENT

Tough times continued. The government came out with a program to give canned beef to those who needed it. I went to Guymon ten miles away to sign up. When I got home, I told Lil, "Oh no! When I was putting down David Lee's birth date, I put 1933 instead of 1934! They'll think he was born out of wedlock!" I hadn't really made that mistake, but I loved to stir Lil up. It worked great. She went into orbit.

But the joke backfired. They sent a worker to investigate the applicants. The moment the woman walked in our door, Lil began to explain my "mistake": "My husband put down...but we were married in...and David Lee was really born in...I have his birth certificate...." And on and on. All the time I was sitting to one side, my face growing redder and redder. I learned a lesson: I was a bit more cautious about telling my wife fibs after that.

We did get some free canned beef. It was good.

OUR FIRST BLACK DUST STORM

Drought conditions had continued for some time, resulting in what was called "The Dust Bowl." The Dust Bowl included all of the Panhandle of Oklahoma (where we lived), some of northwestern Oklahoma, the northern part of Texas, the southern part of Colorado, and some of southern Kansas. We had been in dust storms previous to April of 1935, but that was our first experience with a genuine black "Dust Bowl" dust storm.

One day Lil sat down and wrote up an account of this storm—and those that followed. I'll turn the floor over to her:

> One sunny Sunday afternoon, April 5, 1935, Dave H., our beautiful six-months-old son David, and I were walking home from a friend's place. We were about three blocks from home when we noticed an ominous fearful-looking, rolling, boiling, reddish-black cloud on the horizon. The cloud was moving toward us with terrific speed.
>
> I was frightened and started walking very fast, but Dave H., who was carrying David, stayed calm. I'd run ahead, then go back again. Back and forth I

ran until we reached the door of the house and started down the stairs to our apartment.

Suddenly the cloud enveloped us. It was so dark that you couldn't see your hand in front of your face. The only other place I've seen such darkness was in Carlsbad Caverns. Dave H. turned the light on. We could barely see to go downstairs to our apartment.

The people who lived upstairs came right behind us since the basement was the safest place in the house.

We covered our noses with damp cloths. We put David in his crib, put a cloth over his face and partly covered his crib with a sheet. He would pull the cloth from his face and I would put it back. He would laugh, thinking it was a game.

The darkness lasted for two or three hours. Cars had to stop where they were and wait for the darkness to dispel. When the darkness started to lift, it was dusky with a reddish tint. You could move about if you were careful.

The fourteen-year-old son of the people who owned the apartment house was about two hundred feet from the house when the dust storm hit. He crawled and tried to find his way home. When he could finally see where he was, he found that he was about two hundred yards past his house.

Our apartment had three small windows (about 18" X 30"). All around the windows, the walls were covered with fine black dust. The floor was also covered with this fine dark powder.

This was the first of many such black dust storms. Often, the storms came at night while we were asleep. When we awoke, the only white spot on our pillows was where our heads had lain. We kept David's crib covered with a sheet, so his bed didn't have as much dust on it.

During the day, I covered the big bed (the one Dave H. and I slept in) with newspapers. I would carefully shake dust from one newspaper to the one underneath until it was all on one newspaper which I would gingerly remove from the bed.

It was quite a chore to clean the entire apartment.

If we ate during a storm, I cooked the food in a pot, covered it, and served the food from the pot.

There were dust storms in other places, but none that compared with the ones in the Dust Bowl.

THE WPA

I need to say a few words about the WPA, which was created by President Roosevelt and authorized by Congress in 1935. According to an old joke, "WPA" stood for "We Piddle Around." But the initials originally stood for the Works Progress Administration (later changed to the Works Projects Administration).

Roosevelt's "New Deal" agency was designed to provide work during a time of massive unemployment. It was the most innovative of the president's programs; it was also the most controversial.

Those in charge of the WPA sat around thinking up ways they could put people to work. Among other things, the WPA built thousands of public buildings and facilities. (Our part of the world is dotted with old stone buildings with cornerstones announcing "Built by the WPA" in such and such a year.) WPA workers also built country (dirt) roads—with shovels. Papa couldn't get a job with the WPA even though he was dirt-poor because he had a farm (the mortgaged-to-the-hilt 40-acre home place) and kids who could work.

VISITING LIL'S FOLKS

We generally managed to go home a time or two during the year to see our families. When we visited in Lil's parents' home, as a rule they gathered together in the evening to read the Bible. It was a bit unusual for me to see a *man* take the spiritual lead in his home. Lil's Dad, "Dee," had a painful eye condition, and he sometimes asked me to do the reading. Before I would finish, he would generally get me to read passages like these:

> Mark 16:15, 16—And he said unto them, Go ye into all the world, and preach the gospel to every creature. He that believeth and is baptized shall be saved; but he that believeth not shall be damned.

> Acts 2:36–38—Therefore let all the house of Israel know assuredly, that God hath made that same Jesus, whom ye have crucified, both Lord and Christ. Now when they heard this, they were pricked in their heart, and said unto Peter and to the rest of the apostles, Men and brethren, what shall we do? Then Peter said unto them, Repent, and be baptized every one of you in the name of Jesus Christ for the remission of sins, and ye shall receive the gift of the Holy Ghost.

I later learned that the tricky rascal could quote these and hundreds of other passages from memory.

DAVID STARTS TO COLLEGE

During the fall semester, a child psychology class "borrowed" David Lee to demonstrate infant response. The principle to be demonstrated was simple: Let a child play with a toy, then take it away from him, and he will cry. David turned out to be a poor subject. When they took the toy from him, he laughed. *Whatever* they did, he laughed.

His mother has often proudly stated that her oldest son "started to college at twelve months of age."

20

UNCERTAIN TIMES 1936

Franklin Delano Roosevelt was re-elected in a landslide. Jesse Owens broke two track records at the Olympic games in Germany. The Volkswagen made its appearance. Robert Redford was born. Top radio shows included the Kate Smith show and the Green Hornet. In Oklahoma, the 16th Legislature was called into session. Working on social reform, it became known as "The Spending 16th."

UNCERTAINTY AT GOODWELL

Loys and I thought we had it made at Panhandle A & M since Byron was president. However he had been appointed to that position by governor "Alfalfa" Bill Murray, and the man Murray backed to succeed him had been defeated in November of 1934. It was only a matter of time until Byron got his walking papers, and sure enough that happened. I had my college job until summer but I wasn't sure what I would do after that.

In the spring of 1936, I made the PAMC Livestock Judging Team. We got a free trip to the Fort Worth Livestock Show where we represented the college in the judging competition. Underline the word "free." That trip of five-hundred-plus miles was an adventure for us young men. One or two of us could sing and we sang "You Are My Sunshine" all the way there and back. That song by Jimmie Davis, governor of Louisiana, was the only one all of us knew. One of our team members—"Bearcat" Swinburn—was the comic of the bunch; he kept us laughing with his crazy antics. We didn't win top honors in the competition, but we did receive special recognition.

One of the highlights of the trip was staying in a hotel in downtown Fort Worth. Another highlight was that each of us had his picture made with a fat man. (It didn't take much to entertain us.) I got my one college letter for being part of that team.

A SUMMER IN CORDELL

When school was out, since Byron was no longer president, we decided there was no need to spend the summer in Goodwell. We headed to southwest Oklahoma where Lil's folks lived. We lived in a two-room house in Cordell, Oklahoma, for a week. That's one time we ran out of food; we were down to a few dried prunes. But Lil's dad brought us a few groceries. Then we heard about a man who wanted a couple to stay with him and another man to cook for them (both their wives had left them). We lived there two weeks, Lil cooking in exchange for our meals. Then one of the wives came back and we had to move again. "Move" usually didn't mean much more than shifting our suitcase from one spot to another.

This time we rented the back of a house. The house had a back porch with a back yard David could play in. Lil would sit on the back porch and smile while she watched her one-and-a-half-year-old play. One day she looked up for a moment. When she looked back, he was gone! The ice man (the guy who brought blocks of ice to your house) came along about that time. He stopped his deliveries and helped her search. The house was a block from the county court-house. They finally found David on the far side of the courthouse, in his training pants, talking to strangers and making them laugh. Lil couldn't see anything funny about the situation. After that, she never took her eyes off David while he was playing.

I got a job with a crew that was black-topping roads in the area. I got it because one of Lil's brother-in-laws was crew chief—and because Byron pulled some strings. It was a boiling-hot summer—one of the hottest on record—and I got a job as a flag man directing traffic. I had seen flag men before and thought, "That's the job to have! Just stand around all day and get paid for it!" I disliked it as much as any job I ever had! But they paid me $60.00 a month. That was big bucks in those days. We lived on half of it and saved the other half. Maybe I shouldn't mention it, but the crew spent their lunch break shooting dice. I admit to losing a nickel or two but I really didn't have the money or the desire for the pastime.

WHERE TO GO?

As fall approached and the time came for college to start again, with Byron gone from PAMC, I didn't know what to do. I still had a year to go before I got my B. S. degree plus I wanted to be a vo-ag (vocational agriculture) teacher which would take additional time. Loys and I hitchhiked to Stillwater, Oklahoma, and applied for jobs at Oklahoma A & M and then hitchhiked home. Lousy trip—took us several days to travel the 150 miles there and back. Lousy results—we weren't offered any jobs. Loys and Nova headed to California with Nova's parents, but Lil and I decided to head back to PAMC. Dad repaired his old car and we loaded our few belongings in it and started to Goodwell to throw ourselves on the mercy of the new president, Ed Morrison.

When I talked to President Morrison, he said all the "good jobs" were gone (the federally-funded $17.40-a-month student jobs like I had had) and all that was left were locally-funded $10.00-a-month jobs. I took one. I kept doing what I had done in earlier years; I just got paid less.

When we first got back to Goodwell, we moved into an old hotel downtown where some of the students lived. This cost $9.00 a month which left $1.00 a month to live on. A girl we knew, Nellie Trimble, said her parents had a two-room furnished house we could rent for $6.00 a month. Hey, that would leave $4.00 a month to live on. So, after two weeks in the hotel, we moved into the little house. We had natural gas (the gas bill was part of the rent) and a two-burner hotplate (no oven). No electricity, but we had a coal-oil lamp. No water in the house, but the owner lived next door and let us get water from his outside hydrant (just part of the perks). Other than the brief stay in the hotel, we lived a whole school year in that house, something of a record for us.

By the time school started, it was obvious Lil was pregnant again. We wanted more children but had kinda planned to wait on number two until I graduated. But we were excited.

After classes began, I was again selected to be on the livestock judging team. In the fall of 1936, the team was scheduled to go to Kansas City for another judging contest. This time, however, each team member had to pay $15.00 to go. $15.00 Lil and I didn't have. So someone else went in my place.

We got a ride home for Christmas. We stayed at Dill but also managed a short visit with my folks. We got David a little rocking chair for Christmas.

21

SECOND CHILD! FIRST JOB!
MORE DUST!
1937

Amelia Earhart disappeared over the South Pacific. Nylon was patented by Dupont.
Jane Fonda and Bill Cosby were born. Disney released his first full-length animated
cartoon: **Snow White and the Seven Dwarfs**. *One of the top radio shows was "The*
Inner Sanctum." Oklahoma continued to struggle with the Depression. In the state,
86,524 persons were employed in 1,284 WPA projects.

MORE DUST

January 1937, we headed back to Goodwell. Some friends of ours, George and
Emily Carpenter, needed a cheaper place to stay, so we sublet one of our two
rooms to them for $3.00 a month. Now we had $7.00 a month to live on!

In the spring, Guymon had a pioneer day. One of Lil's nephew-in-laws got me
a job working as a busboy in a café. I never worked so hard in my life. I didn't
pick up dishes at the tables; I just stayed in the kitchen at the sink and others
brought them to me. I washed dishes from dawn to dusk. I made $2.50.

It was soon evident to all that Lil was pregnant. She was having some serious
health problems and the doctor strongly advised us to make this our last child. Lil
took for granted that it was a little girl and began making frilly dresses. David
talked constantly about his "baby sister." But being a manly kinda guy (130
pounds on a 5' 11" frame), I knew it had to be another boy.

The Dust Bowl was in full swing. My wife says this was the year of...

> ...the worst dust storms on record during the days of the Dust Bowl. Dave H.
> kept the record and it was almost unbelievable. For five days in a row, the vis-
> ibility didn't get much better than twenty feet and usually much less than ten

feet. The dust was as fine as face powder and seemed to come in through the walls. We stuffed old socks and strips of cloth in every crack and put masking tape over that—and it still came in.

Women and children were dying from dust pneumonia. Lil was already having health problems, and David started running a low fever every afternoon. The doctor advised Lil to take David and go somewhere else for the remainder of her pregnancy. They traveled by train to Dill City to stay with her parents. Soon after they arrived, David came down with dust pneumonia. The night his fever finally broke, Lil came down with the same ailment and was very ill. The Dacus' family doctor told Lil's dad to call me. Her folks didn't have a phone but the telephone office was located in the house across the street.

George Carpenter loaned me a Model T coupe he had bought for $10.00 and I started for Dill. George, who was something of a mechanical genius, had rigged the carburetor to burn coal oil (10¢ a gallon) instead of gasoline (15¢ a gallon). Only problem was that I ran out of coal oil and had to put gasoline in it...and that vehicle *drank* gasoline.

Lil was *very* ill for two or three weeks. I was worried. At one point, I didn't take off my clothes for seven days and nights. The doctor came every day to see her (doctors of today, pay attention). She got better shortly before the baby came.

OUR NEW SON!

About April 25, Lil's labor pains started. After a while, her dad called the doctor and he traveled the ten miles from Cordell. Then the pains stopped and he went back to Cordell. Lil was embarrassed.

On May 12, the pains started again. Lil wouldn't let us call the doctor for a long time; she didn't want to be embarrassed again. Finally, about 5:30 p.m., she told her dad to call the doctor. He went across the street to the telephone office. When he got the doctor, the MD asked, "Is she making a fuss?" My father-in-law said, "No, but she won't." "Yes, she will," said Doc. "We have plenty of time. I'll be out after I visit the hospital and have a bite to eat."

In the meantime, Lil's water had broken. I tried my best to stretch the delivery out until the doctor got there. I kept saying, "Wait a minute, Lil! Wait a minute, Lil! Wait a minute, Lil!" But Lil thought she had waited long enough. The baby started coming. I had delivered farm animals babies and had been present when David was born, so had a general idea what I should do. Lil had a hard time, and there was a lot of blood. But finally I held our baby in my hands. I said, "It's another boy, Lil!" I held him up the heels until he took his first breath and cried. I gave a big sigh of relief.

In the meantime, Lil's seventy-year old father had kept the road hot between his house and the telephone office—trying to get hold of the doctor. Finally he got him: "Get yourself out here! The baby's already here!" The neighbor lady (the telephone operator) and I were discussing what to do about the umbilical cord when the doctor arrived. He had the honor of cutting the cord. It's probably just as well that Lil's Goodwell doctor advised us only to have two children. The trauma of having just two boys almost did me in.

We named the new baby Coy Dee. Lil's sister Alma came up with "Coy" (I think someone in the community had that name) and "Dee" was after Lil's father: Byron Decalb, "Dee" for short. He was ten pounds and eleven ounces. A lot of baby for a little mama.

Since Lil had lost so much blood, the doctor advised her to remain very still for several weeks. We found out much later that her uterus had ruptured during the delivery and the prolonged bed rest caused her internal organs to grow together (forming adhesions) which resulted in serious health problems for years. But at the moment, both of us were thrilled to have another healthy young boy. It didn't take David long to switch from "my baby sister" to "my baby brother."

GRADUATION AND A JOB

When Coy was a couple of days old, I headed back to PAMC in the Carpenter's car to finish the semester and get my degree. A friend, Herman Humphreys, traveled back with me. At one point on the trip, we were speeding along at 10 or 15 mph when one of the rear wheels came off. We stopped, found the wheel and the nut, put everything back together, and continued on our way.

Shortly after I got back, I had a message from a friend, Mr. Stewart. He was a man of retirement age who had been in charge of the college farm during Byron's regime. The previous year he had taught in a school in Edler, Colorado, but he was leaving and thought I could get the job. If you look at a map, you'll see that the lower right-hand corner of Colorado borders the left top end of the panhandle of Oklahoma. Edler was tucked away in that lower right-hand corner of Colorado.

After classes were out on Friday afternoon, a friend Furn Hooker and I got a ride with another student who lived not far from Edler. We rode with him to Campo, Colorado, about six miles from Edler. We called the Stewarts from a store. While waiting to be picked up, I went to the outhouse behind the store. It was dark, cold, windy, and dusty. After taking care of business, I was running back to the shelter of the store—and hit a clothes line. It caught me in the throat and my feet went flying up. A shocker!

The Stewarts took us home with them. The next day I met with the school board and they hired me to be the principal of the two-room school. My salary would be $85.00 a month! Quite a step up from the $10.00 a month we had been getting! For that salary, I would teach, be the principal, be the janitor, and build the fires in the winter.

A few days later, May 19, 1937, I got my BS degree in Agriculture with a minor in Science. Dad sent me a new suit for graduation. I think he was proud of his oldest boy graduating from college!

I got a job working full-time for the college during the summer. A couple of weeks later, the first of June, Lil came by train to Goodwell with David and new baby Coy. The trip from Sayre to Goodwell took twenty-seven hours. Lil was thin and pale, but I was glad to see her and my two sons!

We bought our first car: a 1930 Chevy coupe. Info for youngsters: A coupe had one seat and a large trunk called a turtle. Someone had removed the turtle in our coupe and had installed a little bed (wooden box) for hauling things. We paid about $130 for the car, most of it on credit with monthly payments of $10.00. We were in high cotton: I had a new son, a college degree, a car, and a teaching job! In the middle of the Depression!

We took a trip in our "new" car to Dill City and Stratford to see our folks before we headed to Colorado. Grandpa Hampy had had a stroke a few months before and was bedfast. His right side was paralyzed and he could barely talk. He still enjoyed the children. David would sit by the side of his bed and he would pat his head. He had us lay Coy on his bed so he could play with him. We stayed two or three days. That was the last time we saw Grandpa. He died a few months later.

We went back to Goodwell. About August 1, we gathered up what household goods we had. Dad and Oren gave us a almost-new three-burner coal-oil cook stove they weren't using. Everything we had fit in the back of the little coupe. The shelf behind the seats was used as a bed for our boys. One would sleep on the shelf and the other would sleep on the seat between us. We traveled the hundred or so miles to Edler without incident.

EDLER, COLORADO

Edler was a nearly deserted little town about twenty-five miles from the county seat of Springfield—mainly south, but a little east. Edler had two general stores; the post office was located in one of them. The town was in the middle of the Dust Bowl. There were no crops or pasture. Most of the farmers had moved away. Here's my wife (the DB expert) again:

> The land looked desolate. One day there would be a high sand dune in one place and, the following day, it would be somewhere else. We always kept a shovel in our car to shovel the dirt out of the road so we could get through. Our yard was bare ground with piles of fine dirt here and there. The soil was dark and rich, but it could not produce without water.
>
> The farm west of our house had been a large wheat farm. The farm house, just a mile from our house, had a fence with a gate. Only the top twelve inches of the fence and gate could be seen above the dirt. The entire farm was like that: bare ground and huge piles of dirt here and there. The farm had several huge barns and a number of combines near the house. All deserted. It made me sad to look at that farm.
>
> The dust storms continued while we were at Edler. When we saw them coming, we'd cover everything as best we could. The storms could last a day or more or just a few hours. After they were over, we'd clean the dirt out of the window sills, sweep the walls, shake the dust out of the curtains, and then take the covers off the bed and furniture.

You could see a few old cows in pastures. Farmers (the few who were left) cut Russian thistles and stacked them for hay. Russian thistles don't have much nutritional value but they will grow anywhere. Ever see a tumble weed? That's a dead, dry Russian thistle.

Edler had seen better days, but we didn't care. We weren't used to much—and I had a job!

LIVING HIGH

In Edler, we rented a three-room house close to the school for $10.00 a month. It was comfortable—and large by our standards. A three-room house for just the four of us! It had a combination living room and dining room, a small bedroom, and a small kitchen. We had a cistern under the house that held water. The kitchen had a sink and a pitcher pump (a little hand pump) on the cabinet. Running water inside the house!

For those who don't know, a cistern is not the same as a well. Water seeps into a well but you have to *put* water in a cistern. It is just a storage tank. About a mile and a half from our house, the postmaster had a windmill with a water tank. Every Saturday I loaded a 50 gallon barrel on the back of my whoopee (i.e., car), went to the tank, and filled the barrel with water. After I brought it back to the house, I used a hose to siphon the water into the cistern under the house. A little muscle on the kitchen pump and we had running H2O!

(Yes, we also had the usual outside "path" for basic needs. And a No. 2 washtub for inside baths.)

Since we were now affluent, we bought a few pieces of new furniture from the Montgomery Ward catalogue, and repaired and painted some used furniture. Our house was soon outfitted with a small table and chairs, a duo fold, a bed, the little cook stove my folks had given us, and other stuff. We even bought a new gas-powered washing machine (our house did not have electricity).

Did I hear someone ask, "What's a duo fold?" A duo fold was a couch whose back could be let down so that it made a bed—similar to present day U.S. futons. This was our "extra bed" for company. Our duo fold was a cheap model and one of our first visitors was a woman who weighed at least 300 pounds. We held our breath when she settled herself on our new duo fold—but it passed the test.

We also had a coal-burning stove in the living-dining room for heat. I bought coal in 100# bags at one of the general stores. About once a month we went to Springfield. Any way you look at it, we were living high.

MY FIRST TEACHING JOB

I was ready for the next big adventure in my life: my first teaching job!

The WPA was building a rock two-classroom schoolhouse with a basement, but it wasn't quite ready when time came for school to start. Classes began in a tar-paper shack on the corner of the school grounds. We moved into the new building in about two weeks.

Since it was a two-room school, we had two teachers. (Have I mentioned I was top dog—the *principal?*) The other teacher was Mrs. "Buddy" Hodges, wife of a local rancher, who had several years experience. She taught grades one through four while I had grades five through eight. We also had one high school girl (9th grade; the nearest high school was twenty miles and she had no transportation). We curtained off a little spot for our high schooler and found an old typewriter and typing book for her. She took two classes: typing and English.

We also had a cook who served lunch in the basement each day at noon. Free—paid for by the government. Lots of soup and beans. Meat was scarce, but I had no complaints. We ran two school buses—well, two school cars. We had a total of about twenty-two children.

Since this was my first teaching job, I admit I was apprehensive. I only had a dozen or so kids but I was nervous. Nervous? I was scared to death! The first day, somehow I made it through the morning. But in the middle of the afternoon, three-year old David walked into my room with his "school books" and sat down in one of the seats. He was sitting quietly so I decided to let him stay. But when I turned my head, he grabbed my bell (my symbol of principal-ship) and rang it as loudly as he could. Embarrassing!

By and large, my class got off to a good start. I had a minor incident the first week. A 6th grade boy brought his knife and starting carving his initials on one of the desks—a common pastime in schoolrooms of the day. I gave him my best "teacher frown" and asked, "Are you planning to buy that desk?" Startled, he shook his head "No." I took the knife from him and gave it back to him at the end of the school day. I had no more trouble with desk carving.

We seldom had visitors to class, but one day the County Superintendent showed up: a pretty young woman. She took a seat and told me to continue; she was just there to observe. I gulped. I wanted so badly to make a good impression. I wondered what I was going to do. Then I had A Thought. It was time for 5th and 6th grade history. "Get out your history books," I said to the 5th and 6th graders, "and turn to page so and so." The session started out great—until one of my smart-aleck students said, "But Mr. Roper, we had this lesson yesterday!" Another red-faced moment. That was the only time the County Superintendent visited our school that year.

The new WPA school building doubled as a community building. There was a folding door between the two classrooms and a little stage in my room so the entire building could be opened and used for community activities. The local Grange (Colorado farmer's organization) met there. They also put on a Negro minstrel show—now politically incorrect but enjoyed back then.

A word or two about a "hot" issue might be in order here: As best I can remember, I had seen a total of four black people at that point in my life. Lots of Indians lived where we lived but no African-Americans. Court houses had segregated drinking fountains and restrooms but I hadn't seen half of them being used. Yes, I had heard crude expressions of racial prejudice, but survival—not segregation—had been high on my family's list of priorities during my growing up years.

But back to the Grange: They once sponsored a community dance, but that evidently got pretty wild. The next morning, I saw a school board member picking up whiskey bottles and unmentionables off the school ground. That was the last community dance.

NO SPIRITUAL PROGRESS

There was no church in Edler, so we were back in religious limbo. But one incident highlighted my spiritual shortcomings: We were invited to eat with a family in the community. Before we started eating, the host asked *me* to "say the blessing." Someway I mumbled and stumbled through it. Embarrassing!

Christmas of 1937, we went back to Oklahoma for a visit. We went with Wilson and Stella Lancaster. Wilson and Stella had been in my graduating class at Lake Valley High School. They were teaching in a one-room school about six miles from us and living in a dugout. They couldn't ride with us since our coupe only had one seat, so we rode with them.

22

CAN'T GET ENOUGH
SCHOOLING
1938

Kate Smith sang "God Bless America" for the first time. A popular song was titled "Flat Foot Floozies With a Floy Floy." American panicked over the radio broadcast of H. G. Wells, "War of the Worlds." The Biro brothers patented the ballpoint pen. The Fair Labor Act established a minimum wage (40 cents an hour) and set the work week at 44 hours. The Nazis captured Austria without a struggle. In Oklahoma, Leon "Red" Phillips ran for governor with a campaign centered around economy. He was elected as the eleventh governor of the state.

ENOUGH IS ENOUGH

The winter of 37–38 was bitter cold in Edler, Colorado. Antifreeze was basically unheard of. Some put alcohol in their radiators to keep them from freezing, but we couldn't afford that. I had to drain the water from the car every time after I used it. One night I didn't, and the block froze and broke. (I did the same thing in Oklahoma the first winter after I learned to drive. I'm a slow learner.)

Lil was not well. Soon after school had started, we had hired one of our eighth-grade girls, Alice Findley, to stay with us and help Lil with the work (the girl worked for her board). Later, Alice's cousin, Mary Ellen Findley, took her place. "Buddy," the other teacher, had to be gone several weeks to care for her sick mother and Lil had to substitute for her. We hired an 18-year-old neighborhood girl to take care of our boys while Lil taught. Lil kept getting thinner.

Our four-year-old David had a really bad case of the croup. Croup was scary and dangerous, especially when you had no doctors, hospitals, or drug stores nearby. David suffered one attack after another, always at night. Finally someone gave us a home remedy: Take a piece of fat pork about an inch square. Spear the meat with a fork and hold it over the flame of a coal-oil lamp. Catch the drippings in a spoon and give it to the patient. It worked! It's about the only thing that did work on David's croup.

During the winter, Coy also got sick—with pneumonia. We had to call the doctor from Springfield. At the time we didn't know everything that was involved in our family's health problems, but we figured the cold winter and dust storms weren't helping.

In the spring, we had two graduates from the 8th grade: Alice Findley and Pearl Hiner. The Edler school board wanted to renew my contract for another year. And another school in the county offered both Lil and me a job in a two-room school. But we had had enough of the dust and cold. The folks of Edler had been extra nice to us, but when I got the opportunity to go back to college, we couldn't resist.

Lil's brother Byron wrote that I could get a job as a graduate assistant at Oklahoma A & M in Stillwater. (Look at the map. Stillwater was *not* in the Dust Bowl!) I would teach two classes on general agriculture to prospective Oklahoma teachers. (In those days, all Oklahoma teachers had to have at least one college course in agriculture to get their teaching certificate; Oklahoma was, after all, an agricultural state. I would have one class of freshmen and sophomores and one class of juniors and seniors. Both classes would study a 6th–7th grade textbook on agriculture.) At the same time, I could work on my certificate to teach vocational agriculture. If I couldn't buy my farm right away, at least I could teach about farming and I could work with farmers.

BACK TO OKLAHOMA

June 1938, we packed up and drove to Lil's folks' place in Dill City, Oklahoma. After a couple of weeks, I worked out a deal with Bill Leonard who had a country store west of Dill. We moved into a two-room furnished apartment beside the store.

I took over an ice route from Lil's brother Zeke. Each morning I would drive fifteen miles in my modified coupe to the ice plant in Cordell. They would put three 300# blocks of ice in the bed of my car. They just fit—but the rear springs of my small car complained a little. I would then start the route Zeke had established. For the youngsters out there: The forms in which the ice was frozen put grooves in the big blocks so you could chip off the size you wanted. Most folks used a 25# or 50# chunk. At each home, I would chip off what they wanted and then carry the ice with ice tongs into their homes where I put it in their ice boxes. Not refrigerators, but ice boxes: upright food storage cabinets with a compartment for ice.

When I finished the route, I headed back to Bill's store and put the left-over ice in a wooden box Bill had; the box slowed the melting of the ice. I sat by the box and sold ice to folks who stopped by. By the end of the day, I generally sold all the ice.

I also fixed flats. There weren't many, but Bill let me keep the money from that. If I needed to be somewhere else, Bill would sell ice for me. If Bill wanted to be gone, I watched the store for him—pumping gas and the like. In return, Bill let us live in the little apartment for free. It was a good arrangement for both of us.

Near the end of the summer, we made a trip back to Colorado to pick up what we had left there. Then we headed for Stillwater. On our way, we stopped at Gracemont, where Dad and Oren were living on a farm. Oren decided that my 13-year-old brother Troy needed to move to Stillwater with us. She packed his suitcase and tied it on top of our stuff.

Our apartment in Stillwater was on Knoblock Street, two blocks south of the campus. It had a fair-sized living room, a small kitchen, a small bedroom, and a private bath. Our landlady Mrs. Cunningham was not happy about five of us living there. And Troy was miserable. He was a great kid, but he missed the farm. Finally Lil's Dad sent money for the train fare and Troy went back to Gracemont. He just lived with us two weeks.

I was paid $50.00 a month as a graduate assistant. That was the good news. The bad news was that our apartment cost $25.00 a month. We struggled to live on the left-over $25.00. Fortunately groceries were fairly cheap and Lil soon had the boys bubbling over with good health (and a little mischief, but I won't mention that). We stayed in the Cunningham apartment until Christmas.

I mentioned earlier that Dad sent me a new suit for my graduation from PAMC. That suit had worked overtime in Edler. Then Lil finished it off one day in Stillwater when she was pressing the pants—and burned a hole in them. Lil's brother Henry gave me a pair of his trousers to finish out the year.

BACK IN CHURCH

The church of Christ in Stillwater met in a little white building. They had around hundred members. Wilbur Hill was the preacher. When Lil and I moved to Stillwater, Wilbur and Susie Hill gave us special attention. They even had us into their home for a meal. They got us attending regularly. According to Lil, even when she was ill, I would take the boys to Bible class. Maybe so.

During the Christmas break, we made a trip home. We had told David that Santa didn't have much money that year. He said, "I just want some funny papers and a ball that bounces." He got both.

23

SHADES OF THE GRAPES OF WRATH!
1939

Three classic movies hit the screen: "Mr. Smith Goes to Washington," "The Wizard of Oz," and "Gone With the Wind." Burns and Allen were the stars of one of the most popular radio shows. World War II began in Europe when Hitler's troops invading Poland. Great Britain and France declared war on German and Italy. In Oklahoma, the Depression had been almost as hard on the state as on the citizens. In January of 1939, the state deficit was over $25 million.

We needed more money to live on. When we returned to Stillwater after the holidays, we rented a two-bedroom house and rented one bedroom to two girls. They had access to the kitchen. That didn't work out, so we only stayed there a couple of months. In April, we moved to a basement apartment. We weren't there long. Then we moved into a basement with Loys and Nova Lee.

I mentioned earlier that the Lees had headed to California the fall of '36. Loys had been working in California for the past two years, but had decided to finish his degree as an industrial-arts teacher. He and Nova came to Stillwater for his final year. So we were near these special friends again. Our families were growing. We had David and Coy and the Lees had two daughters: Darlene and Phillys.

BAPTIZED

In April of '39, the church of Christ had a gospel meeting. The preacher's name was C. E. McGaughey. As I've said, I was raised to believe in God—and the revival meetings of my childhood had impressed on me there was a heaven and a hell. This plus Lil's example and the teaching I was hearing at church services made me increasingly conscious of my spiritual needs. Today I would say that I was becoming aware of the sin of my life and that I needed God's grace to remove my guilt. Back then, if I had said anything (which was unlikely), I would proba- bly have said that I knew I needed to "do something." Anyway, not far into the meeting, after one of the sermons, I responded to the invitation and was bap- tized. I still had a *long* way to go spiritually, but it was a major milestone. And one thing about it, it made Lil one happy mama!

NO JOB? BUT I HAVE A CERTIFICATE!

I finished the summer session of school at Oklahoma A & M about the first of August 1939, qualifying for my certificate to teach vo-ag in Oklahoma. It takes about 124 hours to get a bachelor's degree. By the time I had my certificate, I had 210 hours.

But I couldn't get a job. I had two interviews but was not hired at either place. There were more vo-ag teachers than there were jobs for vo-ag teachers. I tried to get a regular teaching job, but had no luck there either. School boards figured that as soon as I had a chance to teach vo-ag, I would leave them high and dry. About August 1, I gave up. We packed what we could in the back of my whoopee and left the rest with a professor, Chris White. We headed back to Dill—again—to live with Lil's elderly parents. We stayed with them from August to October.

A few weeks after we got there, it was cotton picking time. I patched an old cotton sack and got a job pulling bolls. I got fifty cents per hundred pounds. In good cotton, I could pull 400–500 pounds or more a day. The cotton crop was so sorry that year that I did well to pull 200–300 pounds. Here I was with a teaching certificate, with one year teaching experience, plus another year and summer of college, and qualified to teach vo-ag—and I was pulling bolls for $1.00–$1.50 per day. But we were eating.

About the end of September, cotton was getting scarce and I got a job to help a man head feed. He was going to pay me $1.25 per day; I had to furnish my own lunch. "Heading feed" = cutting the heads off kafir corn with a knife and throw- ing the heads in a wagon. The stalks were left in the field.

The evening before I was to start this lucrative new job, my cousin, Garvin Rakestraw, his wife Bonnie, and their daughter Anita came by to spend the night. They were on their way back to California. Garvin gave me a glowing report about his job in northern California: He was working on a dam near Redding,

California, making $10.00 a day. He was sure I could get a job, too, if I wanted to go out there. Hmmm. $1.25 a day vs. $10.00 a day. Which should I choose? Lil and I had a family conference. I wanted to go with Garvin, get a job, and then send for the family. Lil had other ideas: I wasn't going anywhere without her and the boys!

The next morning, we packed a few clothes, loaded into Garvin's car and headed west to the Land of Opportunity. There were seven of us in the car: four adults and three children. We left our car (which was about worn out) and the rest of our belongings at the Dacus' place. I never heard what happened to the man and his kafir corn.

After you've been married to the same woman seventy years, you know what buttons to push to get a desired reaction. If I want Lil to turn a lovely shade of purple, all I have to do is mention the book *The Grapes of Wrath*. After smoke stops boiling from her ears, she starts to sputter: "*Somebody* ought to write the story of the Dust Bowl the way it *really* was! Steinbeck had no idea what he was talking about! He even got mixed up on his locations!" But Steinbeck got this much right: Lots of folks from Dust Bowl areas headed west looking for relief.

"THINGS GOT WORSE"

There's an old joke: "A guy told me to cheer up; things could get worse. So I cheered up, and he was right. Things got worse." Originally, that wasn't a joke. The man who said it was an Okie who tried to make it in California.

Three days after leaving western Oklahoma, we arrived at Garvin and Bonnie's place. We were a long way from home—1600 or so miles—a fair piece for a cotton-pickin' Okie. Garvin and Bonnie lived in a tent house about three miles south of Redding, California. Trailer houses hadn't been invented, but the hills and valleys were covered with tents and tent houses.

Redding was a small town of about 2000 population, situated on the bank of the Sacramento River in Northern California. The river has long been noted for its gold-bearing gravel and salmon fishing. At the time, the government was building a huge dam about fifteen miles above Redding, called the Mount Shasta Dam. The gravel for the concrete was taken from the river bed. It was run through an extracting machine to remove the gold, then placed on the world's longest conveyor belt and moved twelve miles to the dam site.

We stayed with Garvin and Bonnie while we were getting settled. Garvin took me downtown to the Union Hall and help me to join the union. It cost $80.00

to join the union. I had no money so they let me join "on credit." I was supposed to pay them out of my earnings.

Each morning I would walk to town and sit in the Union Hall all day, without lunch, hoping a job would turn up. Usually fifteen or twenty other men were doing the same. Some of them played pinochle all day. I never learned to play the game. Occasionally, someone would come in and everyone would rush to see if any jobs were available. About 5:00 p.m., I would hit the road for tent city. This continued for several weeks.

Lil decided to take the boys to Los Angles to visit her sister Susie. I borrowed bus fare from Garvin and they left. After visiting a few days, some kind of friction arose. Lil wrote me, expressing her *strong* desire to come back. I showed the letter to the union boss. He had a kind heart, I guess, because the next day he placed me as a welder's helper on the extracting machine. I worked on the swing shift, going to work in the afternoon and working until midnight. Wow, I was excited! $10.00 per day! I'd be rich soon!

My job was to watch the man doing the electric welding and see that no sparks set the rubber conveyer belt on fire. They gave me a face shield and told me to avoid looking at the welding arc. I tried but the retinas of my eyes were burned. I was miserable for several days. I just worked on the job ten days.

I got another loan from Garvin and sent for Lil. We continued living with the Rakestraws a few more days until I got my check for the ten days of work. It came. $100.00! Thinking jobs lay on the horizon, I paid my union dues in full ($80.00) and we decided to get our own place.

We went around the hill a quarter of a mile and rented space for a tent house. We bought enough rough lumber for $6.00 to build the frame for our tent (10' x 12'). Our little house had a wooden floor and wooden sides up about three feet. We borrowed an old tent from Garvin to go over the top. In a short time, we finished the construction.

We borrowed bedding and dishes from the Rakestraws and moved into our new home. We carried water from a community well about two hundred yards down the hill. Lil and the boys picked up sticks for a little tin cooking stove we bought for $2.00. It was the rainy season but the weather was mild, so we didn't need a heating stove. Lil tried to make the place homey. She and the boys picked up rocks and lined the path leading to the house. The boys were short on toys but not on imagination. David made mud pies, put them out to dry, and then displayed them in his "store."

I still walked every day to Redding and sat, waiting for a job. After a few more weeks, I got one more day's work: cleaning up the site of an old building that had burned down. The three months we were in California, I worked a total of eleven days. In case you don't have your calculator handy, $110.00 minus $80.00 union dues equals $30.00.

This had to be one of the lowest points of our married life. No job, no car, no money, and hundreds of miles from home. As Christmas approached, five-year-old David worried that Santa Claus wouldn't find us 'way out in California. That worried me, too.

24

OKLAHOMA NEVER LOOKED SO GOOD! 1940

F. D. R. was elected for an unprecedented third term. Winston Churchill was appointed Prime Minister of Great Britain. England was bombed extensively by the German Luftwaffe. Ted Koppel was born. In Oklahoma, the war with Nazi Germany broke the stranglehold of the Depression as the demand for U. S. goods suddenly accelerated.

BACK TO OKLAHOMA

In January 1940, we got a telegram from Lil's brother, Byron: "You have a job teaching vo-ag with S. E. Spann at Liberty Mounds." S. E. Spann had been my college history professor at Panhandle A & M. He had left PAMC when Byron left. Liberty Mounds was an all-twelve-grades country school about ten miles southwest of Bixby, Oklahoma, and just south of Tulsa. The vo-ag teacher at Liberty Mounds had gotten a better job and had left the school in the middle of the school year, so they needed a teacher.

I should say a few words about Byron. You've seen his name again and again in this book: Through his influence, Lil got her first teaching job, I got a job at PAMC, I got a summer job on the road, I got an assistantship at Oklahoma A & M, and now I had a job teaching vo-ag. And he helped us in other ways. Teacher, school administrator (high school superintendent, County Superintendent, and college president), and State Senator (26 years)—quite a guy!

But back to Redding, California: I had the promise of a job but how were we going to get back to Oklahoma? Byron (who else?) helped us get a $50.00 loan from the bank at Dill. My cousin Garvin Rakestraw took us to San Francisco where we made contact with a share-the-ride program. These programs were a product of the Depression. It was expensive to ride the bus. If someone was headed the direction you wanted to go, he would charge you half or less what the bus company would charge.

The next day, we left with our "shared ride" on our way to Phoenix, Arizona. My folks had moved there and Dad was working on a dairy farm. When we got there, Dad worked some on his old Plymouth and decided it would get us to Oklahoma. Hansel, Troy, and Oren would take over his dairy responsibilities while he was gone.

The trip back to Oklahoma was an experience. We had car trouble (generator). It was bitter cold. We barely had enough for gas, so were hungry most of the time (Lil made sure the boys were fed). We spent one night in a dirty, run-down, flea-bag of a motel. My family of four all slept in the same bed to keep from freezing. Dad was probably colder than we, but he wasn't a complainer.

We finally arrived in Dill City. My car had been sitting all the time we were gone and was not drivable. The next day, I left Lil and the boys with her folks and Dad took me to Liberty Mounds to start teaching. My salary was $160.00 a month.

I stayed two weeks with the Spanns. Lil's brother, Zeke, took her and the boys and a trailer to Stillwater to get the furniture we had left there. Then he brought them and our goods to Liberty Mounds.

We rented the front half of a brick house a mile east of the school. A young couple, the Dee Tuttles, rented the back half. The house was big but run-down. We paid $8.00 a month for three rooms. We got our water from a cistern outside. Natural gas came from a nearby oil well and didn't cost us extra. We had a good-sized bedroom, a room we used as a kitchen (the Tuttles had the real kitchen in the back of the house), and a huge living room that swallowed our few pieces of furniture. The Rural Electric Association (the REA) had been started by the government the year before to bring electricity to rural areas, but it took several years for electricity to reach most areas, so we still used coal-oil lamps. We stayed in that house about nine months, until the start of a new school year in the fall.

Shortly after we arrived, we bought a used 1935 Chevy four-door sedan. The nearest church of Christ was in Bixby, and we drove there for services.

TEACHING VO-AG

In January, the second semester began and I started teaching vo-ag. That first Monday morning, I entered my room in the basement of the two-story school building with both excitement and fear. I had taught in the elementary school in Edler one year and had taught prospective teachers for a year, but I had not taught high school students before. My new job required me to teach three classes of agriculture in the morning (boys only in those days). In the afternoons, I was to check on the boys' "home projects"—such as show animals they were raising.

In addition to the classes and projects, I was to visit and work with the farmers in the community. Vo-ag teachers were required to be available to help 365 days a year. Thus, unlike most teaching jobs, vo-ag teachers were not paid for nine month's work each year, but for twelve. The new methods the teachers had learned in school were looked on with suspicion by some farmers, who had no patience with "educated fools" with their "book larnin'." And, with a few farmers, the teachers had to work around doing things "by the moon" and other "signs." In general, however, vo-ag teachers were appreciated by the community.

After school, I would take four or five boys and we would run terrace lines, vaccinate livestock, detail sheep, poison pests (such as prairie dogs), cull hens, and doctor sick farm animals. (I'm not sure I was overly successful at that last task.) On weekends I was available to help and farmers often called me. It was a different kind of teaching and I enjoyed it!

In August, Lil had the first of her major surgeries: a hysterectomy in a Tulsa hospital. She was in the hospital three weeks and had to come home in an ambulance. We hired someone to stay with her the first six weeks she was home.

NOT DOING TOO BADLY

My contract (which went from July 1 to July 1) was renewed. In September, I started my first full school year of teaching vo-ag. I was getting accustomed to, and acquainted with, the community and I looked forward to the new school year.

About the time school started, we moved to a small, weather-beaten, old-as-the-hills wooden house across the road from the school. The house had a screened-in porch (where we slept in the summer) and a back porch with a cistern. West of the house was an old barn. We had a gas light hanging from the living room ceiling. (That's right. A gas light, not electric.) We bought our first radio while living there—battery operated. Since farmers had to be able to get hold of me, we even got a telephone!

Our oldest, David Lee, started to the first grade that fall. According to state regulations, a child had to turn six before September 1 to start in the first grade. David would not have his sixth birthday until the middle of November, but he was big for his age, smart (took after his mother), and had been begging forever to go to school. So they made an exception.

In October of 1940, I had my 27th birthday. As best I can figure, I had moved (including all the moves while in college) over forty times in my twenty-seven years. But my little family and I were doing OK. We had a roof over our heads and a salary sufficient to pay the bills. I didn't have my land yet—and wouldn't for another fourteen years. Not to mention the barn and the horse. But I did have a loving wife and two healthy boys. And a college education and a good job. And my health and a growing faith. I wasn't doing too badly for the son of a sharecropper.

0-595-32106-2

CPSIA information can be obtained at www.ICGtesting.com
Printed in the USA
LVOW08s1043081215

465928LV00001B/195/P